American Diplomatic History
Before 1900

GOLDENTREE BIBLIOGRAPHIES
In American History

under the series editorship of

Arthur S. Link

AMERICAN DIPLOMATIC HISTORY
BEFORE 1900

compiled by

Norman A. Graebner
University of Virginia

AHM Publishing Corporation
Arlington Heights, Illinois 60004

ISBN: 0-88295-543-8, paper
ISBN: 0-88295-573-x, cloth

Library of Congress Card Number: 77-85991

PRINTED IN THE UNITED STATES OF AMERICA
788

Contents

CONTENTS

CONTENTS

Editor's Foreword

Goldentree Bibliographies in American History are designed to provide students, teachers, and librarians with ready and reliable guides to the literature of American history in all its remarkable scope and variety. Volumes in the series cover comprehensively the major periods in American history, while additional volumes are devoted to all important subjects.

Goldentree Bibliographies attempt to steer a middle course between the brief list of references provided in the average text-book and the long bibliography in which significant items are often lost in the sheer number of titles listed. Each bibliography is, therefore, selective, with the sole criterion for choice being the significance—and not the age—of any particular work. The result is bibliographies of all works, including journal articles and doc-toral dissertations, that are still useful, without bias in favor of any particular historiographical school.

Each compiler is a scholar long associated, both in research and teaching, with the period or subject of his volume. All compilers have not only striven to accomplish the objective of this series but have also cheerfully adhered to a general style and format. However, each compiler has been free to define his field, make his own selections, and work out internal organization as the unique demands of his period or subject have seemed to dictate.

The single great objective of *Goldentree Bibliographies in American History* will have been achieved if these volumes help re-searchers and students to find their way to the significant literature of American history.

Arthur S. Link

Preface

Any bibliography designed to be of general use to students and teachers presents special problems of selection. Whereas the listings in this volume are not exhaustive, they are more comprehensive than the reference lists to be found in general textbooks. For that reason the user should find among its some 2000 items those writings which comprise, because of either the information or the interpretations which they convey, the basic literature in the area of American foreign relations before 1900. This bibliography includes, in addition to books and articles, some references to major published sources as well as to several dozen dissertations available on microfilm. The organization of this volume provides for the inclusion of writings on all aspects of United States diplomatic history. Although there are occasional cross references, the user must supplement the listings for any specific subject with an examination of the "Syntheses" and "Surveys" sections of Chapter I as well as the "General Studies" section which introduces the chapter directly involved. Because the general studies for the period 1865–1900 often include information on all aspects of United States foreign relations, the list which introduces Chapter IX on "Hemispheric Relations, 1865–1900," applies as well to the chapters which follow. At any rate, the table of contents and the index of authors should render this bibliography readily useful.

Norman A. Graebner

Abbreviations

Ag Hist	Agricultural History
Ala Hist Q	Alabama Historical Quarterly
Am Econ Rev	American Economic Review
Am Hist Rev	American Historical Review
Am J Int Law	American Journal of International Law
Am Law Rev	American Law Review
Am Lit	American Literature
Am Neptune	American Neptune
Am Pol Sci Rev	American Political Science Review
Am Q	American Quarterly
Am Slavic and E Eur Rev	American Slavic and East European Review
Ann Am Acad Pol Soc Sci	Annals, American Academy of Political and Social Science
Ann Rep Am Hist Assn	Annual Report of the American Historical Association
Atl Mon	The Atlantic Monthly
Bus Hist Rev	Business History Review
Cal ist Soc Q	California Historical Society Quarterly
Can Hist Rev	Canadian Historical Review
Cath Hist Rev	Catholic Historical Review
Chinese Soc and Pol Sci Rev	Chinese Social and Political Science Review
Civ War Hist	Civil War History
Columbia Uni Q	Columbia University Quarterly
Econ Hist Rev	Economic History Review
Eng Hist Rev	English Historical Review
Essex Inst Hist Coll	Essex Institute Historical Collections
Fla Hist Q	Florida Historical Quarterly
Ga Hist Q	Georgia Historical Quarterly
Harper's New Mon Mag	Harper's New Monthly Magazine

ABBREVIATIONS

His Am Hist Rev	Hispanic American Historical Review
His Teach Mag	History Teachers Magazine
Hist Outlook	Historical Outlook
Hunt Lib Q	Huntington Library Quarterly
Ind Mag of Hist	Indiana Magazine of History
Iowa J Hist and Pol	Iowa Journal of History and Politics
J Am Geog Soc of New York	Journal of the American Geographical Society of New York
J Am Hist	Journal of American History
J Am Stud	Journal of American Studies
J Asian Stud	Journal of Asian Studies
J Black Stud	Journal of Black Studies
J Br Stud	Journal of British Studies
J Confl Res	Journal of Conflict Resolution
J Econ and Bus Hist	Journal of Economic and Business History
J Econ Hist	Journal of Economic History
J Ill St Hist Soc	Journal of the Illinois State Historical Society
J Latin Am Stud	Journal of Latin American Studies
J Mex Am Hist	Journal of Mexican American History
J Miss Hist	Journal of Mississippi History
J Mod Hist	Journal of Modern History
J Neg Hist	Journal of Negro History
J Pol Econ	Journal of Political Economy
J S Hist	Journal of Southern History
Jour Q	Journalism Quarterly
La Hist	Louisiana History
Md Hist Mag	Maryland Historical Magazine
Me Hist Soc Coll	Maine Historical Society Collections
Mich Hist	Michigan History
Mid-Am	Mid-America
Mil Affairs	Military Affairs
Minn Hist	Minnesota History
Minn Hist Soc Coll	Minnesota Historical Society Collections
Miss Val Hist Rev	Mississippi Valley Historical Review
Mo Hist Rev	Missouri Historical Review
N Am Rev	North American Review
N Car Hist Rev	North Carolina Historical Review
N Eng Q	New England Quarterly
Nat Geog Mag	National Geographic Magazine

ABBREVIATIONS

NJ Hist	New Jersey History
NY Hist Soc Q	The New York Historical Society Quarterly
Ohio Hist	Ohio History
Ohio St Arch and Hist Q	Ohio State Archaeological and Historical Quarterly
Oregon Hist Q	Oregon Historical Quarterly
Poac Hist Rev	Pacific Historical Review
Pac Northwest Q	Pacific Northwest Quarterly
Pa Hist	Pennsylvania History
Pa Mag of Hist and Biog	Pennsylvania Magazine of History and Biography
Pol Sci Q	Political Science Quarterly
Proc Am Antiquarian Soc	Proceedings, American Antiquarian Society
Proc Am Philos Soc	Proceedings, American Philosophical Society
Proc Leeds Philos Soc	Proceedings of the Leeds Philosophical and Literary Society
Proc Mass Hist Soc	Proceedings, Massachusetts Historical Society
Proc Miss Val Hist Assn	Proceedings, Mississippi Valley Historical Association
Proc US Naval Inst	Proceedings, United States Naval Institute
Proc Wis Hist Soc	Proceedings, Wisconsin Historical Society
Pub Buffalo Hist Soc	Publications, Buffalo Historical Society
Pub S Hist Assn	Publications, Southern Historical Association
Pub E Tenn Hist Soc	Publications, East Tennessee Historical Society
Q J Econ	Quarterly Journal of Economics
Rev of Rev	Review of Reviews
Rev Pol	Review of Politics
S Atl Q	South Atlantic Quarterly
S Car Hist Mag	South Carolina Historical Magazine
Sat Rev	Saturday Review
Sci Soc	Science and Society
Soc Stud	Social Studies
Southern Cal Q	Southern California Quarterly

ABBREVIATIONS

Southern Q	Southern Quarterly
Southwest Pol and Soc Sci Q	Southwest Political and Social Science Quarterly
Southwestern Hist Q	Southwestern Historical Quarterly
Southwestern Soc Sci Q	Southwestern Social Science Quarterly
Tenn Hist Q	Tennessee Historical Quarterly
Tex Q	The Texas Quarterly
Trans Royal Hist Soc	Transactions of the Royal Historical Society
Trans Royal Soc Can	Transactions of the Royal Society of Canada
Va Mag of Hist and Biog	Virginia Magazine of History and Biography
Va Q Rev	Virginia Quarterly Review
Ver Hist	Vermont History
W Pol Q	Western Political Quarterly
Washington Hist Q	Washington Historical Quarterly
Western Hist Q	Western Historical Quarterly
Wm and Mary Q	William and Mary Quarterly
World Aff Q	World Affairs Quarterly
Wor Pol	World Politics
Yale Rev	Yale Review

NOTE: Cross references are to item numbers. Items marked by an asterisk (*) are available in paperback. The publisher and compiler invite suggestions for additions to future editions of the bibliography.

I. General References

1. Bibliographies, Guides, Historiography

1 BEMIS, Samuel Flagg, and Grace Gardner GRIFFIN, eds. *Guide to the Diplomatic History of the United States, 1775—1921.* Washington, 1935.

2 CONOVER, Helen F. *A Guide to Bibliographic Tools for Research in Foreign Affairs.* 2d ed. Washington, 1958.

3 Council on Foreign Relations. *Foreign Affairs Bibliography.* 4 vols. New York, 1933—1964.

4 DeCONDE, Alexander. *New Interpretations in American Foreign Policy.* Washington, 1961. Historiographical pamphlet.

5 DENNIS, Donnie Lee. "A History of American Diplomatic History." Doctoral dissertation, University of California, Santa Barbara, 1971.

6 *Dissertation Abstracts: A Guide to Dissertations and Monographs Available in Microfilm.* Ann Arbor, Mich., 1952— .

7 FREIDEL, Frank, ed. *Harvard Guide to American History.* Rev. ed. Cambridge, Mass., 1974.*

8 GRIFFIN, Grace Gardner, *et al. Writings on American History, 1902— .* Washington, 1905— .

9 HANDLIN, Oscar, *et al,* eds. *Harvard Guide to American History.* Cambridge, Mass., 1954.*

10 HOWE, George F., *et al. The American Historical Association's Guide to Historical Literature.* New York, 1960.

10A KUEHL, Warren F., ed. *Dissertations in History: An Index to Dissertations Completed in History Departments of United States and Canadian Universities, 1873—1960.* Lexington, Ky., 1965.

11 NEU, Charles E. "The Changing Interpretive Structure of American Foreign Policy." *Twentieth-Century American Foreign Policy.* See **66.**

12 TRASK, David F., Michael C. MEYER, and Roger R. TRASK, comps. and eds. *A Bibliography of United States-Latin American Relations Since 1810: A Selected List of Eleven Thousand Published References.* Lincoln, Nebr., 1968.

2. Documents

13 ADAMS, Charles Francis, ed. *The Works of John Adams.* 10 vols. Boston, 1856.

GENERAL REFERENCES

14 *American State Papers: Foreign Relations.* 6 vols. Washington, 1832–1859. Diplomatic documents, 1789–1828.

15 BARTLETT, Ruhl J., ed. *The Record of American Diplomacy.* 4th ed. New York, 1964.

16 BOYD, Julian P., ed. *The Papers of Thomas Jefferson.* Princeton, N.J., 1950–.

17 BURNETT, Edmund Cody, ed. *Letters of Members of the Continental Congress.* 8 vols. Washington, 1921–1936.

18 BUTTERFIELD, Lyman H., ed. *The Diary and Autobiography of John Adams.* 4 vols. Cambridge, Mass., 1961.

19 BUTTERFIELD, Lyman H., ed. *Adams Family Correspondence.* Cambridge, Mass., 1963–.

20 DE PAUW, Linda Grant, ed. *Documentary History of the First Federal Congress of the United States of America, March 4, 1789–March 3, 1791.* Baltimore, 1972–.

21 DONIOL, Henri. *Histoire de la Participation de la France à l'establissement des États–Unis d'Amerique: Correspondance diplomatique et documents.* 5 vols. Paris, 1886–1892.

22 FERRELL, Robert H., ed. *America as a World Power, 1872–1945.* Columbia, S.C., 1971.*

23 FITZPATRICK, J. C., ed. *The Writings of George Washington.* 39 vols. Washington, 1931–1941.

24 FORD, Paul Leicester, ed. *The Writings of Thomas Jefferson.* 10 vols. New York, 1892–1899.

25 FORD, Worthington C., ed. *The Writings of John Quincy Adams.* 7 vols. New York, 1913–1917.

26 GRAEBNER, Norman A., ed. *Ideas and Diplomacy: Readings in the Intellectual Tradition of American Foreign Policy.* New York, 1964.

27 HACKWORTH, Green H. *Digest of International Law.* 8 vols. Washington, 1940–1944.

28 HAMILTON, John C., ed. *The Works of Alexander Hamilton.* 7 vols. New York, 1850–1851.

29 HAMILTON, S. M., ed. *The Writings of James Monroe.* 7 vols. New York, 1898–1903.

30 HUNT, Gaillard, ed. *The Writings of James Madison.* 9 vols. New York, 1900–1910.

31 HUTCHINSON, William T., and Robert A. RUTLAND, eds. *The Papers of James Madison.* Chicago, 1962–.

32 ISRAEL, Fred L., ed. *Major Peace Treaties of Modern History, 1648–1967.* 4 vols. New York, 1967.

33 JENSEN, Merrill, ed. *The Documentary History of the Ratification of the Constitution.* Madison, Wis., 1976–.

34 JOHNSON, Henry P., ed. *Correspondence and Public Papers of John Jay.* 4 vols. New York, 1890–1892.

35 LINK, Arthur S., and William M. LEARY, Jr., eds. *The Diplomacy of World Power: The United States, 1889–1920.* New York, 1970.*

36 MANNING, William R., ed. *Diplomatic Correspondence of the United States Concerning the Independence of the Latin-American Nations.* 3 vols. New York, 1925.

37 MANNING, William R., ed. *Diplomatic Correspondence of the United States: Inter-American Affairs, 1831– 1860.* 12 vols. Washington, 1932– 1939.

38 MANNING, William R., ed. *Diplomatic Correspondence of the United States-Canadian Relations, 1784– 1860.* 4 vols. Washington, 1940– 1945.

39 MILLER, David Hunter, ed. *Treaties and Other International Acts of the United States of America.* 8 vols. Washington, 1931 –.

40 MOORE, John Bassett. *A Digest of International Law.* 8 vols. Washington, 1906.

41 MOORE, John Bassett. *History and Digest of International Arbitrations.* 6 vols. Washington, 1898.

42 RAPPAPORT, Armin, ed. *Sources in American Diplomacy.* New York, 1966.*

43 RICHARDSON, James D., ed. *A Compilation of the Messages and Papers of the Presidents.* 11 vols. New York, 1914.

44 SMITH, Daniel M., ed. *Major Problems in American Diplomatic History: Documents and Readings.* Boston, 1964.

45 SMYTH, Albert H., ed. *The Writings of Benjamin Franklin.* 10 vols. New York, 1905– 1907.

46 SPARKS, Jared, ed. *The Diplomatic Correspondence of the American Revolution.* 12 vols. Boston, 1829– 1830.

47 SYRETT, Harold C., ed. *The Papers of Alexander Hamilton.* New York, 1961 –.

48 United States Department of State. *Papers Relating to the Foreign Relations of the United States, 1861 –.* Washington, 1862 –.

49 WHARTON, Francis, ed. *The Revolutionary Diplomatic Correspondence of the United States.* 6 vols. Washington, 1889.

50 WHITEMAN, Marjorie M. *Digest of International Law.* 14 vols. Washington, 1963– 1970.

51 WILLIAMS, William A., ed. *The Shaping of American Diplomacy: Readings and Documents in American Foreign Relations, 1750– 1955.* 2 vols. Chicago, 1970.*

3. Syntheses and Broad Interpretations

52 ADAMS, Ephraim D. *The Power of Ideals in American History.* New Haven, Conn., 1913.

53 ADAMS, Randolph G. *A History of the Foreign Policy of the United States.* New York, 1939.

54 ADLER, Selig. *The Isolationist Impulse: Its Twentieth-Century Reaction.* New York, 1957.*

GENERAL REFERENCES

55 BAILEY, Thomas A. "America's Emergence as a World Power: The Myth and the Verity." *Pac Hist Rev*, XXX (1961), 1 – 16.

56 BAILEY, Thomas A. *A Diplomatic History of the American People.* 9th ed. New York, 1974.

57 BAILEY, Thomas A. *Essays Diplomatic and Undiplomatic of Thomas A. Bailey.* Ed. Alexander DeConde and Armin Rappaport. New York, 1969.

58 BARTLETT, Ruhl J. *Policy and Power: Two Centuries of American Foreign Relations.* New York, 1963.*

59 BEARD, Charles A., and George H. E. SMITH. *The Idea of National Interest: An Analytical Study in American Foreign Policy.* New York, 1934.*

60 BELOFF, Max. "American Foreign Policy and World Power: 1871 – 1956." *British Essays in American History.* Ed. H. C. Allen and C. P. Hill. New York, 1957.

61 BEMIS, Samuel Flagg. "American Foreign Policy and the Blessings of Liberty." *Am Hist Rev*, LXVIII (1962), 291 – 305.

62 BEMIS, Samuel Flagg. *American Foreign Policy and the Blessings of Liberty, and Other Essays.* New Haven, Conn., 1962.

63 BEMIS, Samuel Flagg, ed. *The American Secretaries of State and Their Diplomacy.* 10 vols. New York, 1927 – 1929.

64 BEMIS, Samuel Flagg. *A Diplomatic History of the United States.* 5th ed. New York, 1965.

65 BLAKE, Nelson M., and Oscar T. BARCK, Jr. *The United States in Its World Relations.* New York, 1960.

66 BRAEMAN, John, Robert H. BREMNER, and David BRODY, eds. *Twentieth-Century American Foreign Policy.* Columbus, Ohio, 1971.

67 COLE, Wayne S. *An Interpretive History of American Foreign Relations.* Rev. ed. Homewood, Ill., 1973.*

68 COMBS, Jerald A., ed. *Nationalist, Realist, and Radical: Three Views of American Diplomacy.* New York, 1972.* Readings.

69 DAVIS, Robert Ralph, Jr. "Republican Simplicity: The Diplomatic Costume Question, 1789 – 1867." *Civ War Hist*, XV (1969), 19 – 29.

70 DeCONDE, Alexander, ed. *Isolation and Security.* Durham, N.C., 1957.

71 DeCONDE, Alexander. *A History of American Foreign Policy.* 2d ed. New York, 1971.

72 EKIRCH, Arthur A., Jr. *Ideas, Ideals, and American Diplomacy: A History of Their Growth and Interaction.* New York, 1966.*

73 ELLIS, L. Ethan. *A Short History of American Diplomacy.* New York, 1951.

74 FENSTERWALD, Bernard, Jr. "The Anatomy of American 'Isolationism' and Expansionism." *J Confl Res*, II (1958), 111 – 139, 280 – 309.

75 FERRELL, Robert H. *American Diplomacy: A History.* 2d ed. New York, 1969.

76 FISH, Carl Russell. *American Diplomacy.* New York, 1915.

77 GARDNER, Lloyd C., Walter F. LaFEBER, and Thomas J. McCORMICK. *Creation of the American Empire: U.S. Diplomatic History.* Chicago, 1973.

78 GOEBEL, Julius. *The Recognition Policy of the United States.* New York, 1915.

GENERAL REFERENCES

79 GRABER, Doris A. *Crisis Diplomacy: A History of U.S. Intervention Policies and Practices.* Washington, 1959.

80 GRAEBNER, Norman A., ed. *An Uncertain Tradition: American Secretaries of State in the Twentieth Century.* New York, 1961.*

81 HALLE, Louis J. *Dream and Reality: Aspects of American Foreign Policy.* New York, 1959.

82 HENKIN, Louis. *Foreign Affairs and the Constitution.* Mineola, N.Y., 1972.

83 HOLT, W. Stull. *Historical Scholarship in the United States and Other Essays.* Seattle, Wash., 1967.

84 JULIEN, Claude. *America's Empire.* New York, 1971.*

85 KAPLAN, Lawrence S. "The Brahmin as Diplomat in Nineteenth Century America: Everett, Bancroft, Motley, Lowell." *Civ War Hist,* XIX (1973), 5–28.

86 KENNAN, George F. *American Diplomacy, 1900–1950.* Chicago, 1951.*

87 LATANÉ, John H. *A History of American Foreign Policy.*

88 LEOPOLD, Richard W. *The Growth of American Foreign Policy.* New York, 1962.

89 MAGDOFF, Harry. *The Age of Imperialism.* New York, 1969.

90 MERLI, Frank J., and Theodore A. WILSON, eds. *Makers of American Diplomacy, from Benjamin Franklin to Henry Kissinger.* New York, 1974.*

91 MOORE, John Bassett. *American Diplomacy: Its Spirit and Achievements.* New York, 1905.

92 MOORE, John Bassett. *Principles of American Diplomacy.* New York, 1918.

93 MORGENTHAU, Hans J. *In Defense of the National Interest: A Critical Examination of American Foreign Policy.* New York, 1951.

94 NORTHEDGE, F. S., and M. J. GRIEVE. *A Hundred Years of International Relations.* New York, 1972.

95 OLNEY, Richard. "International Isolation of the United States." *Atl Mon,* LXXXI (1898), 577–588.

96 PERKINS, Dexter. *The American Approach to Foreign Policy.* Cambridge, Mass., 1952.

97 PRATT, Julius W. *A History of United States Foreign Policy.* 3d ed. Englewood Cliffs, N.J., 1972.

98 RAPPAPORT, Armin. *A History of American Diplomacy: Closing the Circle.* New York, 1975.*

99 RAPPAPORT, Armin, ed. *Essays in American Diplomacy.* New York, 1967.*

100 SEARS, Louis Martin. *A History of American Foreign Relations.* New York, 1938.

101 SELLEN, Robert W. "National Interests and the Diplomat's Role in Nineteenth Century United States Foreign Policy." *West Georgia College Studies in the Social Sciences,* XI (1972), 1–9.

102 SMITH, Daniel M. *The American Diplomatic Experience.* Boston, 1972.*

103 TANNENBAUM, Frank. *The American Tradition in Foreign Policy.* Norman, Okla., 1955.

104 VAN ALSTYNE, Richard W. *American Diplomacy in Action.* Stanford, Cal., 1947.

105 VAN ALSTYNE, Richard W. "The Significance of the Mississippi Valley in American Diplomatic History, 1686–1890." *Miss Val Hist Rev*, XXXVI (1949), 215–238.

106 VEVIER, Charles. "American Continentalism: An Idea of Expansion, 1845-1910." *Am Hist Rev*, LXV (1960), 323–335.

107 WARNER, D. F. *The Idea of Continental Union: Agitation for the Annexation of Canada to the United States, 1849–1893.* Lexington, Ky., 1960.

108 WEINBERG, Albert K. "The Historical Meaning of the American Doctrine of Isolation." *Proc Am Philos Soc*, XXXIV (1940), 539–547.

109 WEINBERG, Albert K. *Manifest Destiny: A Study of Nationalist Expansionism in American History.* Baltimore, 1935.*

110 WILLIAMS, William A. *The Tragedy of American Diplomacy.* New York, 1962.*

111 ZIMMERMAN, James F. *Impressment of American Seamen.* New York, 1925.

4. Surveys of Long-Term Relationships with Other Nations

Canada and Great Britain

112 ALLEN, Harry C. *Great Britain and the United States: A History of Anglo-American Relations, 1783–1952.* New York, 1955.

113 BOURNE, Kenneth. *Britain and the Balance of Power in North America, 1815–1908.* Berkeley, Cal., 1967.

114 BREBNER, John Bartlet. *North Atlantic Triangle: The Interplay of Canada, the United States, and Great Britain.* New Haven, Conn., 1945.

115 BRINTON, Crane. *The United States and Britain.* Rev. ed. Cambridge, Mass., 1948.

116 BROWN, Robert Craig. "Canada in North America." *Twentieth-Century American Foreign Policy.* See 66. Canada and the United States since 1898.

117 CAMPBELL, Alexander E. "The United States and Great Britain: Uneasy Allies." *Twentieth-Century American Foreign Policy.* See 66.

118 CAMPBELL, Charles S. *From Revolution to Rapprochement: The United States and Great Britain, 1783–1900.* New York, 1974.

119 CLARK, William. *Less Than Kin: A Study of Anglo-American Relations.* Boston, 1958.

120 CORBETT, Percy E. *The Settlement of Canadian-American Disputes.* New Haven, Conn., 1937.

121 CRAIG, Gerald M. *The United States and Canada.* Cambridge, Mass., 1968.

122 DAVIS, Forrest. *The Atlantic System: The Story of Anglo-American Control of the Seas.* New York, 1941.

123 KEENLEYSIDE, Hugh L., and Gerald S. BROWN. *Canada and the United States: Some Aspects of Their Historical Relations.* 2d ed. New York, 1952.

124 McINNIS, Edgar W. *The Unguarded Frontier: A History of Canadian-American Relations.* Garden City, N.Y., 1942.

125 NICHOLAS, Herbert. *Britain and the U.S.A.* Baltimore, 1963.

126 NICHOLAS, Herbert. *The United States and Britain.* Chicago, 1975.

127 PELLING, Henry. *America and the British Left: From Bright to Bevan.* New York, 1957.

128 SHOTWELL, James T., ed. *The Relations of Canada and the United States.* 25 vols. New Haven, Conn., 1937—1945.

129 SOULSBY, Hugh Graham. *The Right of Search and the Slave Trade in Anglo-American Relations, 1814— 1862.* Baltimore, 1933.

130 TANSILL, Charles C. *America and the Fight for Irish Freedom, 1866— 1922.* New York, 1957.

131 WILSON, Robert R., *et al. Canada-United States Treaty Relations.* Durham, N.C., 1963.

Europe and Russia

132 ADAMS, Henry M. *Prussian-American Relations, 1775— 1871.* Cleveland, 1960.

133 BAILEY, Thomas A. *America Faces Russia: Russian-American Relations from Early Times to Our Day.* Ithaca, N.Y., 1950.

134 BLUMENTHAL, Henry. *France and the United States: Their Diplomatic Relations, 1789— 1914.* Chapel Hill, N.C., 1970.

135 BRINTON, Crane. *The Americans and the French.* Cambridge, Mass., 1968.

136 CARLSON, K. E. *Relations of the United States with Sweden.* Allentown, Pa., 1921.

137 DeCONDE, Alexander. *Half Bitter, Half Sweet: An Excursion into Italian-American History.* New York, 1971.

138 DULLES, Foster Rhea. *The Road to Teheran: The Story of Russia and America, 1781— 1943.* Princeton, N.J., 1944.

139 FOGDALL, Soren J. M. P. *Danish-American Diplomacy, 1776— 1920.* Iowa City, Iowa, 1922.

140 HILDT, John C. *Early Diplomatic Negotiations of the United States with Russia.* Baltimore, 1906.

141 HUGHES, H. Stuart. *The United States and Italy.* Cambridge, Mass., 1953.

142 JENSEN, Oliver O., ed. *America and Russia: A Century and a Half of Dramatic Encounters.* New York, 1962.

143 KEIM, Jeannette L. *Forty Years of German-American Political Relations.* Philadelphia, 1919.

144 LARRABEE, S. A. *Hellas Observed: The American Experience of Greece, 1775–1865.* New York, 1957.

145 LASERSON, Max M. *The American Impact on Russia: Diplomatic and Ideological, 1784–1917.* New York, 1950.

146 McKAY, Donald C. *The United States and France.* Cambridge, Mass., 1951.

147 SCOTT, Franklin D. *The United States and Scandinavia.* Cambridge, 1950.

148 STOCK, Leo F. "American Consuls to the Papal States, 1797–1870." *Cath Hist Rev,* IX (1929), 233–251.

149 THOMAS, Benjamin P. *Russo-American Relations, 1815–1867.* Baltimore, 1930.

150 WHITE, Elizabeth B. *American Opinion of France: From Lafayette to Poincaré.* New York, 1927.

151 WILLIAMS, William A. *American-Russian Relations, 1781–1941.* New York, 1952.

152 WILLSON, Beckles. *America's Ambassadors to France, 1777–1927: A Narrative of Franco-American Diplomatic Relations.* London, 1928.

Africa and the Middle East

153 BADEAU, John S. *The American Approach to the Arab World.* New York, 1968.

154 FIELD, James A., Jr. *America and the Mediterranean World, 1776–1882.* Princeton, N.J., 1969.

155 GORDON, Leland J. *American Relations with Turkey, 1830–1930: An Economic Interpretation.* Philadelphia, 1932.

156 GRABILL, Joseph L. *Protestant Diplomacy and the Near East: Missionary Influence on American Policy, 1810–1927.* Minneapolis, 1971.

157 HALL, Luella J. *The United States and Morocco, 1776–1956.* Metuchen, N.J., 1971.

158 HUREWITZ, Jacob C., ed. *Diplomacy in the Near and Middle East: A Documentary Record.* 2 vols. Princeton, N.J., 1956.

159 SCOTT, William Randolph. "A Study of Afro-American and Ethiopian Relations: 1896–1941." Doctoral dissertation, Princeton University, 1971.

160 SPEISER, Ephraim A. *The United States and the Near East.* Cambridge, Mass., 1950.

161 THOMAS, Lewis V., and Richard N. FRYE. *The United States and Turkey and Iran.* Cambridge, Mass., 1951.

162 YESELSON, Abraham. *United States-Persian Diplomatic Relations, 1883–1921.* New Brunswick, N.J., 1956.

Asia and the Pacific

163 BATTISTINI, Lawrence H. *The United States and Asia.* New York, 1955.

164 BORG, Dorothy, ed. *Historians and American Far Eastern Policy.* New York, 1966. A pamphlet of six essays.

165 CLYDE, Paul H., ed. *United States Policy Toward China: Diplomatic and Public Documents, 1838– 1939.* Durham, N.C., 1940.

166 COHEN, Warren I. *America's Response to China: An Interpretive History of Sino-American Relations.* New York, 1971.*

167 DAVIES, John Paton, Jr. *Dragon by the Tail: American, British, Japanese and Russian Encounters with China and One Another.* New York, 1972.

168 DENNETT, Tyler. *Americans in Eastern Asia: A Critical Study of the Policy of the United States with Reference to China, Japan, and Korea in the 19th Century.* New York, 1922.

169 DULLES, Foster Rhea. *America in the Pacific: A Century of Expansion.* Boston, 1932.

170 DULLES, Foster Rhea. *China and America: The Story of Their Relations Since 1784.* Princeton, N.J., 1946.

171 DULLES, Foster Rhea. *Forty Years of American-Japanese Relations.* New York, 1937.

172 DULLES, Foster Rhea. *Yankees and Samurai: America's Role in the Emergence of Modern Japan, 1791– 1900.* New York, 1965.

173 FAIRBANK, John K. *The United States and China.* Rev. ed. Cambridge, Mass., 1971.*

174 GRATTAN, C. Hartley. *The United States and the Southwest Pacific.* Cambridge, Mass., 1961.

175 GRISWOLD, A. Whitney. *The Far Eastern Policy of the United States.* New York, 1938.*

176 GRUNDER, Garel A., and William E. LIVEZEY. *The Philippines and the United States.* Norman, Okla., 1951.

177 IRIYE, Akira. *Across the Pacific: An Inner History of American-East Asian Relations.* New York, 1967.

178 ISAACS, Harold R. *Scratches on Our Minds: The American Image of China and India.* New York, 1958.

179 Kamikawa, hikomatsu, ed. *Japan-American Diplomatic Relations in the Meiji-Taisho Era.* Trans. Kimura Michiko. Tokyo, 1958.

180 LATOURETTE, Kenneth Scott. *A History of Christian Missions in China.* New York, 1929.

181 LIU, K. C. *Americans and Chinese: A Historical Essay and a Bibliography.* Cambridge, Mass., 1963.

182 MAY, Ernest R., and James C. THOMSON, Jr., eds. *American-East Asian Relations: A Survey.* Cambridge, Mass., 1972. Essays by seventeen specialists.

183 NEUMANN, William L. *America Encounters Japan: From Perry to MacArthur.* Baltimore, 1963.

184 POMEROY, Earl S. "American Policy Respecting the Marshalls, Carolines, and Marianas, 1898 – 1941." *Pac Hist Rev,* XVII (1948), 43 – 53.

185 POMEROY, Earl S. *Pacific Outpost: American Strategy in Guam and Micronesia.* Stanford, Cal., 1951.

186 REISCHAUER, Edwin O. *The United States and Japan.* Rev. ed. Cambridge, Mass., 1965.

187 SCHWANTES, Robert S. *Japanese and Americans: A Century of Cultural Relations.* New York, 1955.

188 SPENCE, Jonathan. *To Change China: Western Advisers in China 1620 – 1960.* Boston, 1969.

189 STEMEN, John Roger. "The Diplomacy of the Immigration Issue: A Study in Japanese-American Relations, 1894 – 1941." Doctoral dissertation, Indiana University, 1960.

190 TOLLEY, Kemp. *Yangtze Patrol: The U.S. Navy in China.* Annapolis, Md., 1971. Covers 1853 – 1942.

191 TOMPKINS, Pauline. *American-Russian Relations in the Far East.* New York, 1949.

192 TUPPER, Eleanor R., and George E. McREYNOLDS. *Japan in American Public Opinion.* New York, 1937.

193 VARG, Paul A. *Missionaries, Chinese and Diplomats: The American Protestant Missionary Movement in China, 1890 – 1952.* Princeton, N.J., 1958.

Latin America

194 BEMIS, Samuel Flagg. *The Latin American Policy of the United States.* New York, 1943.*

195 CALLAHAN, James M. *American Foreign Policy in Mexican Relations.* New York, 1932.

196 CALLCOTT, Wilfred Hardy. *The Western Hemisphere: Its Influence on United States Policies to the End of World War II.* Austin, Tex., 1968.

197 CLINE, Howard F. *The United States and Mexico.* Rev. ed. Cambridge, Mass., 1963.*

198 CONNELL-SMITH, Gordon. "The United States and the Caribbean: Colonial Patterns, Old and New." *J Latin Am Stud,* IV (1972), 113 – 122. A review article.

199 DUGGAN, Laurence. *The Americas: The Search for Hemispheric Security.* New York, 1949.

200 EALY, Lawrence O. *Yanqui Politics and the Isthmian Canal.* University Park, Pa., 1971. Covers the years 1840 – 1970.

201 EVANS, H. C., Jr. *Chile and Its Relations with the United States.* Durham, N.C., 1927.

202 FONER, Philip S. *A History of Cuba and Its Relations with the United States.* 2 vols. New York, 1962—1963.

203 GANTENBEIN, J. W., ed. *The Evolution of Our Latin-American Policy: A Documentary Record.* New York, 1950.

204 HART, Albert Bushnell. *Monroe Doctrine: An Interpretation.* Boston, 1916.

205 HILL, Lawrence F. *Diplomatic Relations Between the United States and Brazil.* Durham, N.C., 1932.

206 HUNDLEY, Norris, Jr. *Dividing the Waters: A Century of Controversy Between the United States and Mexico.* Berkeley, Cal., 1966.

207 INMAN, Samuel Guy. *Inter-American Conferences 1826—1954: History and Problems.* Washington, 1965.

208 JENKS, Leland Hamilton. *Our Cuban Colony: A Study in Sugar.* New York, 1928.

209 KANE, William Everett. *Civil Strife in Latin America: A Legal History of U.S. Involvement.* Baltimore, 1972.

210 KARNES, Thomas L., ed. *Readings in the Latin American Policy of the United States.* Tucson, Ariz., 1972.

211 KNIGHT, Melvin M. *The Americans in Santo Domingo.* New York, 1928.

212 LANGLEY, Lester D. *The Cuban Policy of the United States: A Brief History.* New York, 1968.*

213 LANGLEY, Lester D. *Struggle for the American Mediterranean: United States—European Rivalry in the Gulf-Caribbean, 1776—1904.* Athens, Ga., 1974.

214 LATANÉ, John H. *The United States and Latin America.* Garden City, N.Y., 1920.

215 LIEUWEN, Edwin. *U.S. Policy in Latin America: A Short History.* New York, 1965.

216 LISS, Sheldon B. *A Century of Disagreement: The Chamizal Conflict, 1864—1964.* Washington, 1965.

217 LOGAN, John A. *No Transfer: An American Security Principle.* New Haven, Conn., 1961.

218 LOGAN, Raymond W. *The Diplomatic Relations of the United States with Haiti, 1776—1891.* Chapel Hill, 1941.

219 MACK, Gerstle. *The Land Divided: A History of the Panama Canal and Other Isthmian Canal Projects.* New York, 1944.

220 MARSH, Margaret C. *The Bankers in Bolivia: A Study in American Foreign Investment.* New York, 1928.

221 MECHAM, J. Lloyd. *A Survey of United States-Latin American Relations.* Boston, 1965.

222 MECHAM, J. Lloyd. *The United States and Inter-American Security, 1889—1960.* Austin, Tex., 1961.

223 MILLETT, Allan R. "The United States and Cuba: The Uncomfortable 'Abrazo,' 1898—1968." *Twentieth-Century American Foreign Policy.* See **66.**

224 MONTAGUE, Ludwell L. *Haiti and the United States, 1714—1938.* Durham, N.C., 1940.

225 MOUNT, Graeme Stewart. "American Imperialism in Panama." Doctoral dissertation, University of Toronto, 1969. Covers the period 1846 – 1968.

226 PARKS, E. Taylor. *Colombia and the United States, 1765 – 1934.* Durham, N.C., 1935.

227 PERKINS, Dexter. *A History of the Monroe Doctrine.* Boston, 1955.*

228 PERKINS, Dexter. *The United States and the Caribbean.* 2d ed. Cambridge, Mass., 1966.

229 PETERSON, Dale William. "The Diplomatic and Commercial Relations Between the United States and Peru from 1883 to 1918." Doctoral dissertation, University of Minnesota, 1969.

230 PETERSON, Harold F. *Argentina and the United States, 1810 – 1960.* Albany, N.Y., 1964.

231 PIERSON, William Whatley, Jr. "The Political Influences of an Inter-Oceanic Canal, 1826 – 1926." *His Am Hist Rev,* VI (1926), 205 – 231.

232 PIKE, Fredrick B. *Chile and the United States, 1880 – 1962: The Emergence of Chile's Social Crisis and the Challenge to United States Diplomacy.* Notre Dame, Ind., 1963.

233 RICHARD, Alfred Charles, Jr. "The Panama Canal in American National Consciousness 1870 – 1922." Doctoral dissertation, Boston University, 1969.

234 RIPPY, J. Fred. *The Capitalists and Colombia.* New York, 1931.

235 RIPPY, J. Fred. *The United States and Mexico.* Rev. ed. New York, 1931.

236 STUART, Graham H. *Latin America and the United States.* New York, 1928.

237 WELLES, Sumner. *Naboth's Vineyard: The Dominican Republic, 1844 – 1924.* 2 vols. New York, 1928.

238 WHITAKER, Arthur P. *The United States and Argentina.* Cambridge, Mass., 1954.

239 WHITAKER, Arthur P. *The United States and South America: The Northern Republics.* Cambridge, Mass., 1948.

240 WHITAKER, Arthur P. *The Western Hemisphere Idea: Its Rise and Decline.* Ithaca, N.Y., 1954.

241 ZORRILLA, Luis G. *Historia de las Relaciones entre México y los Estados Unidos de América 1800 – 1958.* 2 vols. Mexico City, 1965 – 1966.

5. Selected Studies Related to American Diplomatic History

Institutions, Public Opinion, and Practices of Diplomacy

242 BAILEY, Thomas A. *The Man in the Street.* New York, 1948.

GENERAL REFERENCES

243 BAILEY, Thomas A. *The Art of Diplomacy: The American Experience.* New York, 1968.

244 BARNES, William, and John H. MORGAN. *The Foreign Service of the United States: Origins, Development, and Functions.* Washington, 1961.

245 BYRD, Elbert M., Jr. *Treaties and Executive Agreements in the United States: Their Separate Roles and Limitations.* The Hague, 1960.

246 CARROLL, Holbert N. *The House of Representatives and Foreign Affairs.* Pittsburgh, 1958.

247 CORBETT, Percy E. *Law in Diplomacy.* Princeton, N.J., 1959.

248 DAHL, Robert A. *Congress and Foreign Policy.* New York, 1950.*

249 DANGERFIELD, Royden J. *In Defense of the Senate.* Norman, Okla., 1933.

250 DeCONDE, Alexander. *The American Secretary of State: An Interpretation.* New York, 1962.*

251 FARNSWORTH, D. N. *The Senate Committee on Foreign Relations.* Urbana, Ill., 1961.

252 FUCHS, L. H. "Minority Groups and Foreign Policy." *Pol Sci Q*, LXXIV (1959), 161−175.

253 GOULD, J. W. "The Origins of the Senate Committee on Foreign Relations." *W Pol Q*, XII (1959), 670−682.

254 HILL, Norman L. *Mr. Secretary of State.* New York, 1963.

255 HOLT, W. Stull. *Treaties Defeated by the Senate: A Study of the Struggle Between President and Senate over the Conduct of Foreign Relations.* Baltimore, 1933.

256 ILCHMAN, W. F. *Professional Diplomacy in the United States: A Study in Administrative History.* Chicago, 1961.

257 KUEHL, Warren F. *Seeking World Order: The United States and International Organization to 1920.* Nashville, Tenn., 1969.

258 PLISCHKE, Elmer. *United States Diplomats and Their Missions: A Profile of American Diplomatic Emissaries Since 1778.* Washington, 1975.*

259 ROSENAU, James N., ed. *Domestic Sources of Foreign Policy.* New York, 1967.

260 STUART, Graham H. *American Diplomatic and Consular Practice.* 2d ed. New York, 1962.

261 STUART, Graham H. *The Department of State: A History of Its Organization, Procedure, and Personnel.* New York, 1949.

262 WESTPHAL, A. C. F. *The House Committee on Foreign Affairs.* New York, 1942.

263 WILCOX, Francis O. *Congress, the Executive and Foreign Policy.* New York, 1971. On the separation of powers.

264 WRISTON, Henry M. *Executive Agents in American Foreign Relations.* Baltimore, 1929.

Economic Aspects of Foreign Policy

265 CURTI, Merle E., and Kendall BIRR. *Prelude to Point Four: American Technical Missions Overseas, 1838–1938.* Madison, Wis., 1954.

266 DANIEL, Robert L. *American Philanthropy in the Near East, 1820–1960.* Athens, Ohio, 1970.

267 DEUTSCH, Karl W., and Alexander ECKSTEIN. "National Industrialization and the Declining Share of the International Economic Sector, 1890–1959." *Wor Pol*, XIII (1961), 267–299. Statistics on United States foreign trade.

268 ELLIOTT, William Y. *The Political Economy of American Foreign Policy: Report of a Study Group.* New York, 1955.

269 LEWIS, Cleona. *America's Stake in International Investments.* Washington, 1938. Statistics.

270 MADDEN, John T., et al. *America's Experience as a Creditor Nation.* New York, 1937.

271 SNYDER, Richard C. *The Most-Favored Nation Clause.* New York, 1946.

272 TAUSSIG, Frank W. *Tariff History of the United States.* 8th ed. New York, 1931.

Strategy and Military Force

273 ALBION, Robert G., and J. B. POPE. *Sea Lanes in Wartime.* New York, 1942.

274 GRENVILLE, John A. S. "Diplomacy and War Plans in the United States, 1890–1917." *Transactions, Royal Historical Society*, ser. 5, XI (1961), 1–21.

275 GRENVILLE, John A. S., and George Berkeley YOUNG. *Politics, Strategy, and American Diplomacy: Studies in Foreign Policy, 1873–1917.* New Haven, Conn., 1966.

276 HASSLER, Warren W., Jr. *The President as Commander in Chief.* Menlo Park, Cal., 1971.*

277 HUNTINGTON, Samuel P. *The Soldier and the State: The Theory and Politics of Civil-Military Relations.* Cambridge, Mass., 1957.*

278 LIVEZEY, William E. *Mahan on Sea Power.* Norman, Okla., 1947.

279 MAHAN, Alfred Thayer. *From Sail to Steam: Recollections of a Naval Life.* New York, 1907.

280 MILLIS, Walter. *Arms and Men.* New York, 1956.*

281 MILLIS, Walter, et al. *Arms and the State: Civil-Military Elements in National Policy.* New York, 1958.

282 MITCHELL, Donald W. *History of the Modern American Navy from 1883 Through Pearl Harbor.* New York, 1946.

283 O'CONNOR, Raymond G., ed. *American Defense Policy in Perspective: From Colonial Times to the Present.* New York, 1965.*

284 PULESTON, William D. *Mahan: The Life and Work of Alfred Thayer Mahan.* New Haven, Conn., 1939.

285 ROSSITER, Clinton. *The Supreme Court and the Commander-in-Chief.* Ithaca, N.Y., 1951.

286 SAVAGE, Carlton. *The Policy of the United States Towards Maritime Commerce in War, 1776—1914.* Washington, 1934.

287 SPROUT, Harold, and Margaret SPROUT. *The Rise of American Naval Power, 1776—1918.* Princeton, N.J., 1939.*

288 WEIGLEY, Russell F. *The American Way of War: A History of United States Military Strategy and Policy.* New York, 1973.

Peace Movements

289 BROCK, Peter. *Pacifism in the United States from the Colonial Era to the First World War.* Princeton, N.J., 1968.

290 CURTI, Merle E. *Peace or War: The American Struggle, 1636—1936.* New York, 1936.

291 HERMAN, Sondra R. *Eleven Against War: Studies in American Internationalist Thought, 1898—1921.* Stanford, Cal., 1969.*

292 MARCHAND, C. Roland. *The American Peace Movement and Social Reform, 1898—1918.* Princeton, N.J., 1973.

II. Colonial Foundations of American Foreign Relations

1. General Studies

293 BAILEY, Kenneth P. *The Ohio Company of Virginia and the Westward Movement, 1748—1792. A Chapter in the History of the Colonial Frontier.* Glendale, Cal., 1939.

294 BELL, Herbert C. "The West India Trade before the Revolution." *Am Hist Rev,* XXII (1917), 272—287.

295 CLARK, G. N. "War Trade and Trade War, 1701–1713." *Econ Hist Rev*, I (1928), 262–280.

296 CLELAND, Hugh. *George Washington in the Ohio Valley.* Pittsburgh, 1955.

297 CRANE, Verner Winslow. *The Southern Frontier, 1670–1732.* Philadelphia, 1929.

298 CREIGHTON, Donald G. *The Commercial Empire of the St. Lawrence, 1760–1850.* New Haven, Conn., 1937.

299 DAVENPORT, Frances G. *American and European Diplomacy to 1648.* Washington, 1917.

300 DAVENPORT, Frances G. "America and European Diplomacy to 1648." *Ann Rep Am Hist Assn for the Year 1915* (1917), 153–161.

301 DORN, Walter L. *Competition for Empire, 1740–1763.* New York, 1940.

302 ECHEVERRIA, Durand. *Mirage in the West: A History of the French Image of American Society to 1815.* Princeton, N.J., 1957.

303 GIPSON, Lawrence H. *The British Empire before the American Revolution.* 12 vols. New York, 1936–1961.

304 GIRARD, James W. *The Peace of Utrecht.* New York, 1885.

305 GRAHAM, Gerald Sandford. *Empire of the North Atlantic: The Maritime Struggle for North America.* Toronto, 1950.

306 HALSEY, Francis Whiting. *The Old New York Frontier, 1614–1800.* New York, 1901.

307 HASSALL, Arthur. *The Balance of Power, 1715–1789.* London, 1929.

308 HERTZ, G. B. *British Imperialism in the Eighteenth Century.* London, 1908.

309 HIGGINS, Ruth L. *Expansion in New York, with Especial Reference to the Eighteenth Century.* Columbus, Ohio, 1931.

310 HORN, David Bayne, ed. *British Diplomatic Representatives, 1689–1789.* London, 1932.

311 HUNT, George T. *The Wars of the Iroquois.* Madison, Wis., 1940.

312 JOHNSON, Amandus. *The Swedish Settlements on the Delaware: Their History and Relation to the Indians, Dutch and English, 1638–1664.* 2 vols. Philadelphia, 1911.

313 JOHNSON, James G. *The Colonial Southeast, 1732–1763: An International Contest for Territorial and Economic Control. University of Colorado Studies,* XIX. Boulder, Col., 1932.

314 JUDAH, Charles B. *The North American Fisheries and British Policy to 1713.* Urbana, Ill., 1933.

315 LECKY, W. E. H. *History of England in the Eighteenth Century.* 8 vols. New York, 1878–1887.

316 LEDER, Lawrence H. *Robert Livingston 1654–1728 and the Politics of Colonial New York.* Chapel Hill, 1961.

317 LOUNSBURY, Ralph Greenlee. *The British Fishery at Newfoundland, 1634–1763.* New Haven, Conn., 1934.

318 MALCOLM-SMITH, Elizabeth F. *British Diplomacy in the Eighteenth Century.* London, 1937.

319 MERIWETHER, Robert Lee. *The Expansion of South Carolina, 1729–1765.* Kingsport, Tenn., 1940.

320 MINCHINTON, W. E., ed. *The Trade of Bristol in the Eighteenth Century. Bristol Record Society's Publications,* XX (1957).

321 NEWTON, Arthur Percival. *The European Nations in the West Indies, 1493–1688.* London, 1933.

322 NEWTON, Arthur Percival. *A Hundred Years of the British Empire.* London, 1940.

323 NEWTON, Arthur Percival. "The West Indies in International Politics, 1550–1850." *History,* New Series, XIX (1935), 302–310.

324 PALMER, Robert R. *The Age of the Democratic Revolution: A Political History of Europe and America, 1760–1800.* Princeton, N.J., 1959.

325 PARES, Richard. *King George III and the Politicians.* Oxford, Eng., 1953.

326 PARES, Richard. *Colonial Blockade and Neutral Rights, 1739–1763.* Oxford, Eng., 1936.

327 PARES, Richard. *War and Trade in the West Indies, 1739–1763.* Oxford, Eng., 1936.

328 PARGELLIS, Stanley M. *Military Affairs in North America, 1748–1765.* New York, 1936.

329 PEASE, Theodore C., and Ernestine JENISON, eds. *Illinois on the Eve of the Seven Years' War, 1747–1755.* Springfield, Ill., 1940.

330 PECKHAM, Howard H. *Pontiac and the Indian Uprising.* Princeton, N.J., 1947.

331 PENSON, L. M. *Colonial Background of British Foreign Policy.* London, 1930.

332 PETRIE, Sir Charles Alexander. *Earlier Diplomatic History, 1492–1713.* New York, 1949.

333 ROBERTS, Penfield. *The Quest for Security, 1715–1740.* New York, 1947.

334 RULE, J. C. "The Old Regime in America: A Review of Recent Interpretations of France in America." *Wm and Mary Q,* XIX (1962), 575–600.

335 RUSSELL, Nelson Vance. *The British Regime in Michigan and the Old Northwest, 1760–1796.* Northfield, Minn., 1939.

336 SAVELLE, Max. "The American Balance of Power and European Diplomacy, 1713–78." *The Era of the American Revolution: Studies Inscribed to Evarts Boutell Greene.* Ed. Richard B. Morris. New York, 1939.

337 SAVELLE, Max. "The Forty-Ninth Degree of North Latitude as an International Boundary, 1719: The Origin of an Idea." *Can Hist Rev,* XXXVIII (1957), 183–201.

338 SAVELLE, Max. *The Origins of American Diplomacy: The International History of Angloamerica, 1492–1763.* New York, 1967.

339 STRONG, Frank. "Causes of Cromwell's West Indian Expedition." *Am Hist Rev,* IV (1899), 228–245.

340 VINER, Jacob. "Power versus Plenty as Objectives of Foreign Policy in the Seventeenth and Eighteenth Centuries." *Wor Pol,* I (1948), 1–29.

341 VOLWILER, Albert T. *George Groghan and the Westward Movement, 1741–1782.* Cleveland, 1926.

342 WAINWRIGHT, Nicholas B. *George Groghan, Wilderness Diplomat.* Chapel Hill, N.C., 1959.

343 WOLF, John B. *The Emergence of the Great Powers, 1685–1715.* New York, 1951.

2. Anglo-Spanish Rivalry

344 BOLTON, Herbert Eugene, and Mary ROSS. *The Debatable Land: A Sketch of the Anglo-Spanish Contest for the Georgia Country.* Berkeley, Cal., 1925.

345 BROWN, Vera Lee. "Anglo-Spanish Relations in America in the Closing Years of the Colonial Era." *His Am Hist Rev*, V (1922), 329–483.

346 BROWN, Vera Lee. "Studies in the History of Spain in the Second Half of the Eighteenth Century." *Smith College Studies in History*, XV (1929), 3–92.

347 CHRISTELOW, Allan. "Economic Background of the Anglo-Spanish War of 1762." *J Mod His*, XVIII (1946), 22–36.

348 DUNN, William Edward. *Spanish and French Rivalry in the Gulf Region of the United States, 1678–1702: The Beginnings of Texas and Pensacola.* Austin, Tex., 1917.

349 GIPSON, Lawrence H. "British Diplomacy in the Light of Anglo-Spanish New World Issues." *Am Hist Rev*, LI (1946), 627–648.

350 GOLD, Robert L. *Borderland Empires in Transition: The Triple-Nation Transfer of Florida.* Carbondale, Ill., 1969.

351 HILDNER, Ernest C. "The Role of the South Sea Company in the Diplomacy Leading to the War of Jenkins' Ear, 1729–1739." *His Am Hist Rev*, XVIII (1938), 322–341.

352 HUSSEY, Roland D. "Spanish Reaction to Foreign Aggression in the Caribbean to about 1680." *His Am Hist Rev*, IX (1929), 286–302.

353 LANNING, John Tate. "The American Colonies in the Preliminaries of the War of Jenkins' Ear." *Ga Hist Q*, XI (1927), 129–155.

354 LANNING, John Tate. "American Participation in the War of Jenkins' Ear." *Ga Hist Q*, XI (1927), 191–215.

355 LANNING, John Tate. *The Diplomatic History of Georgia: A Study of the Epoch of Jenkins' Ear.* Chapel Hill, N.C., 1936.

356 LAUGHTON, John Knox. "Jenkins' Ear." *Eng Hist Rev*, IV (1899), 742–743.

357 McLACHLIN, Jean O. *Trade and Peace with Old Spain, 1667–1750.* Cambridge, Eng., 1940.

358 NELSON, George H. "Contraband Trade under the Asiento, 1730–1739." *Am Hist Rev*, LI (1945), 55–67.

359 NETTELS, Curtis. "England and the Spanish-American Trade, 1680—1715." *J Mod Hist*, III (1931), 1—33.

360 PEASE, Theodore C. "The Mississippi Boundary of 1763." *Am Hist Rev*, XL (1935), 278—286.

361 REESE, Trevor R. "Georgia in Anglo-Spanish Diplomacy, 1736—1739." *Wm Mary Q*, XV (1958), 168—190.

362 RUSH, N. Orwin. *Spain's Final Triumph over Great Britain in the Gulf of Mexico: The Battle of Pensacola, March 9 to May 8, 1781*. Tallahassee, Fla., 1966.

363 RUSSELL, Nelson Vance. "The Reaction of England and America to the Capture of Havana, 1762." *His Am Hist Rev*, IX (1929), 303—316.

364 TEMPERLEY, Harold W. V. "The Causes of the War of Jenkins' Ear, 1739." *Trans Royal Hist Soc*, III (1909), 198—236.

365 TEMPERLEY, Harold W. V. "Relations of England with Spanish America, 1720—1744." *Annual Report of the American Historical Association for the Year 1911*. 2 vols. I (1913), 229—237.

366 WRIGHT, Irene A., ed. "Spanish Policy toward Virginia, 1606—1612: Jamestown, Ecija, and John Clark of the Mayflower." *Am Hist Rev*, XXV (1920), 448—479.

3. Anglo-Dutch Rivalry

367 CATTERALL, Ralph C. H. "Anglo-Dutch Relations, 1654—1660." *Ann Rep Am Hist Assn for the Year 1910* (1912), 101—121.

368 COHEN, Ronald D. "The Hartford Treaty of 1650: Anglo-Dutch Cooperation in the Seventeenth Century." *NY Hist Soc Q*, LIII (1969), 311—332.

369 DEXTER, F. B. "Early Relations between New Netherland and New England." *Papers of the New Haven Colony Historical Society*, III (1882), 443—469.

370 EDMUNDSON, George. *Anglo-Dutch Rivalry during the First Half of the Seventeenth Century*. Oxford, Eng., 1911.

371 WARD, Christopher. *The Dutch and Swedes on the Delaware, 1609—1664*. Philadelphia, 1930.

4. Anglo-French Rivalry

372 AITON, Arthur S. "Diplomacy of the Louisiana Cession by France to Spain, 1763." *Am Hist Rev*, XXXVI (1931), 701—720.

373 ANDREWS, Charles M. "Anglo-French Commercial Rivalry, 1700—1750: The Western Phase." *Am Hist Rev*, XX (1915), 539—556, 761—780.

374 BAKER-CROTHERS, Hayes. *Virginia and the French and Indian War.* Chicago, 1928.

375 BRADLEY, Arthur Granville. *The Fight with France for North America.* New York, 1900.

376 BURT, A. L. *The Old Province of Quebec.* Toronto, 1933.

377 CALDWELL, Norman Ward. *The French in the Mississippi Valley, 1740—1750.* Urbana, Ill., 1941.

378 CHRISTELOW, Allan. "French Interest in the Spanish Empire during the Ministry of the Duc de Choiseul, 1759—1771." *His Am Hist Rev*, XXI (1941), 517—537.

379 COLE, Charles Woolsey. *Colbert and A Century of French Mercantilism.* 2 vols. New York, 1939.

380 CORBETT, Julian S. *England in the Seven Years War.* 2 vols. London, 1907.

381 CRANE, Verner Winslow. "The Southern Frontier in Queen Anne's War." *Am Hist Rev*, XXIV (1919), 379—395.

382 DRAKE, Samuel Adams. *The Border Wars of New England, Commonly Called King William's and Queen Anne's Wars.* New York, 1897.

383 ECCLES, W. J. *Frontenac, the Courtier Governor.* Toronto, 1959.

384 GIPSON, Lawrence H. "A French Project for Victory Short of a Declaration of War, 1755." *Can Hist Rev*, XXVI (1945), 361—371.

385 GIRAUD, Marcel. *Histoire de la Louisiane Française.* 3 vols. Paris, 1953—1974.

386 HAMER, P. M. "Anglo-French Rivalry in the Cherokee Country, 1754—1757." *N Car Hist Rev*, II (1925), 303—322.

387 HOTBLACK, Kate. "The Peace of Paris, 1763." *Trans Royal Hist Soc*, II (1908), 235—267.

388 LEE, David. "The Contest for Isle aux Noix, 1759—1760: A Case Study in the Fall of New France." *Ver Hist*, XXXVII (1969), 96—107.

389 LODGE, Sir Richard. "The Anglo-French Alliance, 1716—1731." *Studies in Anglo-French History.* Ed. G. A. Coville and H. W. V. Temperley. Cambridge, Eng., 1935.

390 LYON, E. Wilson. *Louisiana in French Diplomacy, 1759—1804.* Norman, Okla., 1934.

391 McLENNON, J. S. *Louisbourg from its Foundation to its Fall.* London, 1958.

392 MIMS, Stewart L. *Colbert's West India Policy.* New Haven, Conn., 1912.

393 MORGAN, William T. "English Fear of 'Encirclement' in the Seventeenth Century." *Can Hist Rev*, X (1929), 4—22.

394 PARKMAN, Francis. *La Salle and the Discovery of the Great West.* Boston, 1896.

395 PARKMAN, Francis. *Count Frontenac and New France under Louis XIV.* Boston, 1877.

396 PARKMAN, Francis. *A Half-Century of Conflict.* 2 vols. Boston, 1894.

397 PEASE, Theodore C., ed. *Anglo-French Boundary Disputes in the West, 1759– 1763.* Springfield, Ill., 1936.

398 RAMSEY, John F. *Anglo-French Relations, 1763– 1770: A Study of Choiseul's Foreign Policy.* Berkeley, Cal., 1939.

399 RASHED, Zenah Esmet. *The Peace of Paris, 1763.* Liverpool, Eng., 1957.

400 ROPES, Arthur R. "The Causes of the Seven Years' War." *Trans Royal Hist Soc,* IV (1889), 143–170.

401 SAVELLE, Max. "Diplomatic Preliminaries of the Seven Years' War in America." *Can Hist Rev,* XX (1939), 17–36.

402 SAVELLE, Max. *The Diplomatic History of the Canadian Boundary, 1749– 63.* New Haven, Conn., 1940.

403 SOSIN, Jack M. "Louisburg and the Peace of Aix-la-Chapelle, 1748." *Wm and Mary Q,* XIV (1957), 516–535.

404 WILSON, Arthur McCandless. *French Foreign Policy during the Administration of Cardinal Fleury, 1726– 1743.* Cambridge, Mass., 1936.

405 WINSOR, Justin. *The Mississippi Basin: The Struggle in America between England and France, 1697– 1763.* Boston, 1898.

406 WRONG, George M. *The Conquest of New France: A Chronicle of the Colonial Wars.* New Haven, Conn., 1918.

407 WRONG, George M. *The Rise and Fall of New France.* 2 vols. New York, 1928.

5. America and British Imperial Policy

408 ALVORD, Clarence W. *The Mississippi Valley in British Politics.* 2 vols. Cleveland, 1917.

409 BEER, George Louis. *British Colonial Policy, 1754– 1765.* Gloucester, Mass., 1958.

410 BROOKE, John. *The Chatham Administration, 1766– 1768.* London, 1956.

411 DICKERSON, Oliver M. *The Navigation Acts and the American Revolution.* Philadelphia, 1951.

412 FEILING, Keith Grahame. *British Foreign Policy, 1660– 1672.* London, 1930.

413 HALL, Hubert. "Chatham's Colonial Policy." *Am Hist Rev,* V (1900), 659–675.

414 HIGHAM, Charles Strachan Sanders. *The Development of the Leeward Islands under the Restoration, 1660– 1688. A Study of the Foundations of the Old Colonial System.* Cambridge, Eng., 1921.

415 HOTBLACK, Kate. *Chatham's Colonial Policy.* London, 1917.

416 KAMMEN, Michael. *Empire and Interest: The American Colonies and the Politics of Mercantilism.* Philadelphia, 1970.*

417 LODGE, Sir Richard. "The Continental Policy of Great Britain, 1740—1760." *History*, XVI (1931—1932), 298—305.

418 METZGER, Charles H. *The Quebec Act. A Primary Cause of the American Revolution.* New York, 1936.

419 REESE, Trevor R. *Colonial Georgia: A Study in British Imperial Policy in the Eighteenth Century.* Athens, Ga., 1963.

420 SCHUTZ, John A. *Thomas Pownall, British Defender of American Liberty: A Study of Anglo-American Relations in the Eighteenth Century.* Glendale, Cal., 1951.

421 SCHUTZ, John A. *William Shirley, King's Governor of Massachusetts.* Chapel Hill, N.C., 1961.

422 SOSIN, Jack M. "The Massachusetts Acts of 1774: Coercive or Preventive?" *Hunt Lib Q*, XXVI (1963), 235—252.

423 SOSIN, Jack M. *Whitehall and the Wilderness: The Middle West in British Colonial Policy, 1760—1775.* Lincoln, Nebr., 1961.

424 TAYLOR, William S., and J. H. PRINGLE, eds. *Correspondence of William Pitt, Earl of Chatham.* 4 vols. London, 1838—1840.

425 WATSON, D. H. "William Baker's Account of the Debate on the Repeal of the Stamp Act." *Wm and Mary Q*, XXVI (1969), 259—265.

426 WEBB, Stephen Saunders. "William Blathwayt, Imperial Fixer: Muddling through to Empire, 1689—1717." *Wm and Mary Q*, XXVI (1969), 373—415.

427 WILLIAMS, Basil. *The Whig Supremacy, 1714—1760. The Oxford History of England.* 2d ed. Oxford, Eng., 1962.

6. *Colonial Attitudes toward International Affairs*

428 BUFFINGTON, A. H. "The Isolationist Policy of Colonial Massachusetts." *N Eng Q*, I (1928), 158—179.

429 CURREY, Cecil B. *Road to Revolution: Benjamin Franklin in England, 1765—1775.* Garden City, N.Y., 1968.

430 GILBERT, Felix. "The English Background of American Isolationism in the Eighteenth Century." *Wm and Mary Q*, I (1944), 138—160.

431 GILBERT, Felix. *To the Farewell Address: Ideas of Early American Foreign Policy.* Princeton, N.J., 1961.

432 JOHNSON, Joseph E. "A Quaker Imperialist's View of the British Colonies in America, 1732." *Pa Mag of Hist and Biog*, LX (1936), 97—130.

433 NEWBOLD, Robert C. *The Albany Congress and Plan of Union of 1754.* New York, 1955.

434 RIGGS, A. R. "Arthur Lee, A Radical Virginian in London, 1768—1776." *Va Mag of Hist and Biog*, LXXVIII (1970), 268—280.

435 RIPPY, J. Fred, and Angie DEBO. "The Historical Background of the American Policy of Isolation." *Smith College Studies in History*, IX (1924), 71 – 165.

436 SAVELLE, Max. "The Appearance of an American Attitude toward External Affairs, 1750 – 1775." *Am Hist Rev*, LII (1947), 655 – 666.

437 SAVELLE, Max. "Colonial Origins of American Diplomatic Principles." *Pac Hist Rev*, III (1934), 334 – 350.

438 SCHLESINGER, Arthur M. *Prelude to Independence. The Newspaper War on Britain 1764 – 1776.* New York, 1958.

439 VAN ALSTYNE, Richard W. *The Rising American Empire.* New York, 1960.*

440 WEINBERG, Albert K. "The Historical Meaning of the American Doctrine of Isolation." *Am Pol Sci Rev*, XXXIV (1940), 539 – 547.

III. The Diplomacy of American Independence

1. General Studies

441 ABERNETHY, Thomas Perkins. *Western Lands and the American Revolution.* New York, 1959.

442 ALVORD, Clarence W. *The Illinois Country, 1673 – 1818.* Springfield, Ill., 1920.

443 AUGUR, Helen. *The Secret War of Independence.* New York, 1955.

444 BEMIS, Samuel Flagg. *The Diplomacy of the American Revolution.* New York, 1935.*

445 BURLINGAME, Roger. *Benjamin Franklin: Envoy Extraordinary.* New York, 1967.

446 BURNETT, Edmund Cody. *The Continental Congress.* New York, 1941.

447 BURT, A. L. *The United States, Great Britain and British North America from the Revolution to the Establishment of Peace after the War of 1812.* New Haven, Conn., 1940.

448 CALLAHAN, North. *Royal Raiders. The Tories of the American Revolution.* Indianapolis, 1963.

449 COX, Isaac J. "The Indian as a Diplomatic Factor in the History of the Old Northwest." *Ohio Arch and Hist Q*, XVIII (1909), 542 – 565.

450 DARLING, A. B. *Our Rising Empire, 1763 – 1803.* New Haven, Conn., 1940.

451 EAST, Robert A. *Business Enterprise in the American Revolutionary Era.* New York, 1938.

452 EDGERTON, H. E. *The Causes and Character of the American Revolution.* Oxford, Eng., 1923.

453 GIPSON, Lawrence H. "The American Revolution as an Aftermath of the Great War for the Empire, 1754 – 1763." *Pol Sci Q,* LXV (1950), 86 – 104.

454 JAMES, W. M. *The British Navy in Adversity. A Study of the War of American Independence.* London, 1926.

455 LOPEZ, Claude Anne. *Mon Cher Papa: Franklin and the Ladies of Paris.* New Haven, Conn., 1966.

456 LOWELL, E. J. "The United States of North America, 1775 – 1782: Their Political Struggles and Relations with Europe." *Narrative and Critical History of America.* Ed. Justin Winsor. 8 vols. Boston, 1884 – 1889.

457 LYMAN, Theodore. *The Diplomacy of the United States: Being an Account of the Foreign Relations of the Country from the First Treaty with France, in 1778, to the Treaty of Ghent, in 1814, with Great Britain.* Boston, 1826.

458 MACKESY, Piers. *The War for America, 1775 – 1783.* Cambridge, Mass., 1964.

459 MAHAN, Alfred Thayer. *Major Operations of the Navies in the War of American Independence.* London, 1913.

460 MONAGHAN, Frank. *John Jay.* New York, 1935.

461 PAULLIN, Charles O. *Diplomatic Negotiations of American Naval Officers, 1778 – 1883.* Baltimore, 1912.

462 PECKHAM, Howard H. *The War for Independence: A Military History.* Chicago, 1958.

463 RITCHESON, Charles R. *The Era of the American Revolution: The Anglo-American Relation 1763 – 1794.* New York, 1969.

464 ROBSON, Eric. *The American Revolution in its Political and Military Aspects, 1763 – 1783.* London, 1955.

465 SCHLESINGER, Arthur M. *The Colonial Merchants and the American Revolution, 1763 – 1776.* New York, 1918.

466 SHY, John. *Toward Lexington: The Role of the British Army in the Coming of the American Revolution.* Princeton, N.J., 1965.

467 STOURZH, Gerald. *Benjamin Franklin and American Foreign Policy.* Chicago, 1954.

468 TRESCOT, W. H. *The Diplomacy of the Revolution: A Historical Study.* New York, 1852.

469 VAN ALSTYNE, Richard W. *Empire and Independence: The International History of the American Revolution.* New York, 1965.*

470 VAN DOREN, Carl. *Benjamin Franklin.* New York, 1938.

471 VAN TYNE, Claude H. *The Loyalists in the American Revolution.* New York, 1902.

472 VER STEEG, Clarence L. *Robert Morris, Revolutionary Financier.* Philadelphia, 1954.

473 WOOD, G. C. *Congressional Control of Foreign Relations during the American Revolution, 1774– 1789.* Allentown, Pa., 1919.

474 WRIGHT, Esmond. *Fabric of Freedom, 1763– 1800.* New York, 1961.

2. British Policy toward America

475 BARNES, G. R., and J. H. OWEN, eds. *The Private Papers of John Earl of Sandwich, First Lord of the Admiralty, 1771– 1782.* 4 vols. London, 1932– 1938.

476 BUTTERFIELD, Herbert. *George III, Lord North and the People.* London, 1949.

477 BUTTERFIELD, Herbert. *George III and the Historians.* London, 1957.

478 GRUBER, Ira D. "The American Revolution as a Conspiracy: The British View." *Wm and Mary Q*, XXVI (1969), 360– 372.

479 HUTSON, James H. "The Partition Treaty and the Declaration of American Independence." *J Am Hist*, LVIII (1972), 877– 896.

480 KETCHUM, Richard M. "England's Vietnam: The American Revolution." *American Heritage*, XXII, No. 4 (1971), 6– 11, 81– 83.

481 LUTNICK, Solomon. *The American Revolution and the British Press, 1775– 1783.* Columbia, Mo., 1967.

482 NAMIER, Sir Lewis, and John BROOKE. *The House of Commons, 1754– 1790.* 3 vols. London, 1964.

483 RITCHESON, Charles R. *British Politics and the American Revolution.* Norman, Okla., 1954.

484 SMITH, Paul H. *Loyalists and Redcoats. A Study in British Revolutionary Policy.* Chapel Hill, N.C., 1964.

485 SPECTOR, Margaret Marion. *The American Department of the British Government, 1768– 1782.* New York, 1940.

486 VAN ALSTYNE, Richard W. *Empire and Independence.* See **469.**

487 VAN ALSTYNE, Richard W. "Europe, the Rockingham Whigs, and the War for American Independence: Some Documents." *Hunt Lib Q*, XXV (1961), 1– 28.

488 VAN ALSTYNE, Richard W. "Parliamentary Supremacy versus Independence: Notes and Documents." *Hunt Lib Q*, XXVI (1963), 201– 233.

489 VAN ALSTYNE, Richard W. "Great Britain, the War for Independence, and the 'Gathering Storm' in Europe, 1775– 1778." *Hunt Lib Q*, XXVII (1964), 311– 346.

490 WILLCOX, William B. "The British Road to Yorktown: A Study in Divided Command." *Am Hist Roev*, LII (1946), 1– 35.

3. French Policy

491 ABERNETHY, Thomas Perkins. "Commercial Activities of Silas Deane in France." *Am Hist Rev*, XXXIX (1934), 477–485.

492 ACOMB, Frances. *Anglophobia in France, 1763– 1789. An Essay in the History of Constitutionalism and Nationalism*. Durham, N.C., 1950.

493 BOYD, Julian P. "Silas Deane: Death by a Kindly Teacher of Treason?" *Wm and Mary Q*, XVI (1959), 165–187, 319–342, 515–550.

494 CORWIN, Edward S. *French Policy and the American Alliance of 1778.* Princeton, N.J., 1916.

495 CORWIN, Edward S. "The French Objective in the American Revolution." *Am Hist Rev*, XXI (1915), 32–61.

496 IRVINE, D. D. "The Newfoundland Fishery: A French Objective in the War of American Independence." *Can Hist Rev*, XIII (1932), 268–284.

497 JUSSERAND, Jean J. "Our First Alliance." *Nat Geog Mag*, XXXI (1917), 518–548.

498 KETCHAM, Ralph L. "France and American Politics, 1763–1793." *Pol Sci Q*, LXXVIII (1963), 198–223.

499 KITE, Elizabeth S. *Beaumarchais and the War of American Independence.* 2 vols. Boston, 1918.

500 LACOUR-GAYET, G. *La Marine Militaire de la France sous le Règne de Louis XV.* Paris, 1902.

501 LACOUR-GAYET, G. *La Marine Militaire de la France sous le Règne de Louis XVI.* Paris, 1905.

502 LASSERAY, Commandant Andre. *Les Français sous les Treize Étoiles, 1775– 1782.* 2 vols. Paris, 1935.

503 MENG, John J. *The Comte de Vergennes: European Phases of His American Diplomacy, 1774– 1780.* Washington, 1932.

504 MENG, John J., ed. *Dispatches and Instructions of Conrad Alexandre Gérard, 1778– 1780.* Baltimore, 1939.

505 MENG, John J. "The Place of Canada in French Diplomacy of the American Revolution." *Bulletin Recherches Hist*, XXXIX (1933), 665–687.

506 MENG, John J. "A Footnote to Secret Aid in the American Revolution." *Am Hist Rev*, XLIII (1938), 791–795.

507 O'DONNELL, William Emmett. *The Chevalier de La Luzerne. French Minister to the United States 1779– 1784.* Bruges, 1938.

508 PERKINS, J. B. *France in the American Revolution.* Boston, 1911.

509 SCOTT, James Brown. *The United States and France: Some Opinions on International Gratitude.* New York, 1926.

510 STINCHCOMBE, William C. *The American Revolution and the French Alliance.* Syracuse, N.Y., 1969.

511 VAN TYNE, Claude H. "French Aid before the Alliance of 1778." *Am Hist Rev*, XXXI (1925), 20–40.

512 VAN TYNE, Claude H. "Influences which Determined the French Government to Make the Treaty with America, 1778." *Am Hist Rev*, XXI (1916), 528–541.

4. Continental Europe and the West Indies

513 ABBEY, Kathryn T. "Spanish Projects for the Reoccupation of the Floridas during the American Revolution." *His Am Hist Rev*, IX (1929), 265–285.

514 ACOMB, Evelyn M., trans. and ed. *The Revolutionary Journal of Baron Ludwig von Closen, 1780–1783.* Chapel Hill, N.C., 1958.

515 BARTON, H. A. "Sweden and the War of American Independence." *Wm and Mary Q*, XIII (1966), 408–430.

516 BENSON, A. B. "Our First Unsolicited Treaty." *American Scandinavian Review*, VII (1919), 43–49.

517 BENSON, A. B. *Sweden and the American Revolution.* New Haven, Conn., 1926.

518 BROWN, Marvin L., trans. and ed. *American Independence through Prussian Eyes. A Neutral View of the Peace Negotiations of 1782–1783.* Durham, N.C., 1959.

519 CARPENTER, W. S. "The United States and the League of Neutrals of 1780." *Am J Int Law*, XV (1921), 511–522.

520 COE, S. G. *The Mission of William Carmichael to Spain.* Baltimore, 1928.

521 CRESSON, W. P. *Francis Dana, A Puritan Diplomat at the Court of Catherine the Great.* New York, 1930.

522 EDLER, Friedrich. *The Dutch Republic and the American Revolution.* Baltimore, 1911.

523 Giddens, p. h. "arthur Lee, First United States Envoy to Spain." *Va Mag of Hist and Biog*, XL (1932), 3–13.

524 GOLDER, Frank A. "Catherine II and the American Revolution." *Am Hist Rev*, XXI (1915), 92–96.

525 HAWORTH, P. L. "Frederick the Great and the American Revolution." *Am Hist Rev*, IX (1904), 460–478.

526 HILDT, John C. *Early Diplomatic Negotiations of the United States with Russia.* See **140**.

527 JAMESON, J. Franklin. "St. Eustatius in the American Revolution." *Am Hist Rev*, VIII (1903), 683–708.

528 LINGELBACH, W. E. "Saxon-American Relations, 1778–1828." *Am Hist Rev*, XVII (1912), 517–539.

529 MADARIAGA, Isabel de. *Britain, Russia and the Armed Neutrality of 1780.* London, 1962.

530 NASATIR, Abraham P. "The Anglo-Spanish Frontier in the Illinois Country during the American Revolution, 1779–1783." *J Ill St Hist Soc*, XXI (1928), 291–358.

531 PATTERSON, A. Temple. *The Other Armada. The Franco-Spanish Attempt to Invade Britain in 1779.* Manchester, Eng., 1960.

532 ROWEGARTEN, J. G. *Frederick the Great and the United States.* Lancaster, Pa., 1906.

533 SCOTT, James Brown, ed. *The Armed Neutralities of 1780 and 1800.* New York, 1918.

5. The Diplomacy of Peacemaking

534 BALDWIN, S. E. "Franklin and the Rule of Free Ships, Free Goods." *Proc Am Antiquarian Soc*, XXV (1915), 345 – 357.

535 BATES, H. B. "Two Bourbon Ministers and Arthur Lee." *His Am Hist Rev*, XIII (1933), 489 – 492.

536 BEMIS, Samuel Flagg. *The Diplomacy of the American Revolution.* See **444**.

537 BEMIS, Samuel Flagg. "Canada and the Peace Settlement of 1782 – 1783." *Can Hist Rev*, XIV (1933), 265 – 284.

538 BEMIS, Samuel Flagg. "The Rayneval Memoranda of 1782." *Proc Am Antiquarian Soc*, XLVII (1937), 15 – 92.

539 BROWN, G. W. "The St. Lawrence in the Boundary Settlement of 1783." *Can Hist Rev*, IX (1929), 223 – 238.

540 BURTON, Clarence M. "The Boundary Lines of the United States under the Treaty of 1782." *Michigan Pioneer and Historical Collections*, XXXVIII (1912), 130 – 139.

541 CHAMBERLAIN, Mellen. "New England's Interest in the Fisheries in 1781." *Proc Mass Hist Soc*, IV (1889), 48 – 54.

542 CHRISTIE, Ian R. *The End of North's Ministry, 1780 – 1782.* London, 1958.

543 FAY, Bernard. "Franco-American Diplomacy and the Treaty of Paris, 1783." *American Catholic Historical Society Record*, XLIV (1933), 193 – 219.

544 HALE, Edward Everett. *Franklin in France.* 2 vols. Boston, 1888.

545 KLINGELHOFER, H. E., ed. "Matthew Ridley's Diary during the Peace Negotiations of 1782." *Wm and Mary Q*, XX (1963), 95 – 133.

546 MORRIS, Richard B. *The Peacemakers: The Great Powers and Independence.* New York, 1965.

547 MURPHY, Orville T. "The Comte de Vergennes, the Newfoundland Fisheries, and the Peace Negotiation of 1783: A Reconsideration." *Can Hist Rev*, XLVI (1965), 32 – 46.

548 PHILLIPS, Paul C. *The West in the Diplomacy of the American Revolution.* Urbana, Ill., 1913.

549 TYLER, Lyon G. "Arthur Lee, A Neglected Statesman." *Tyler's Quarterly Historical and General Magazine*, XIV (1932 – 1933), 65 – 76, 128 – 138, 197 – 216.

550 WEAD, Eunice. "British Public Opinion of the Peace with America, 1782." *Am Hist Rev*, XXXIV (1929), 513—531.

6. Diplomacy under the Articles of Confederation

551 BOYD, Julian P. "Two Diplomats between Revolutions: John Jay and Thomas Jefferson." *Va Mag of Hist and Biog*, LXVI (1958), 131—146.

552 ELLIOT, Jonathan, ed. *The Debates in the Several States Conventions on the Adoption of the Federal Constitution*. Philadelphia, 1891.

553 IRWIN, Ray W. *The Diplomatic Relations of the United States with the Barbary Powers, 1776—1816*. Chapel Hill, N.C., 1931.

554 JENSEN, Merrill. *The New Nation: A History of the United States during the Confederation, 1781—1789*. New York, 1950.

555 KAPLAN, Lawrence S. *Jefferson and France: An Essay on Politics and Political Ideas*. New Haven, Conn., 1967.

556 KEITH, Alice B. "Relaxations in the British Restrictions on the American Trade with the British West Indies, 1783—1802." *J Mod Hist*, XX (1948), 1—18.

557 McLAUGHLIN, Andrew C. "The Western Posts and the British Debts." *Ann Rep Am Hist Assn for the Year 1894* (1895), 413—444.

558 MARKS, Frederick W., III. *Independence on Trial: Foreign Affairs and the Making of the Constitution*. Baton Rouge, 1973.

559 REEVES, Jesse S. "The Prussian-American Treaties." *Am J Int Law*, XI (1917), 475—510.

560 RITCHESON, Charles R. "Anglo-American Relations, 1783—1794," *S Atl Q*, LVIII (1959), 364—380.

561 RITCHESON, Charles R. "The British Press and the First Decade of American Independence." *J Br Stud*, II (1963), 88—109.

562 RITCHESON, Charles R. *Aftermath of Revolution: British Policy Toward the United States, 1783—1795*. Dallas, Tex., 1969.

563 RITCHESON, Charles R. " 'Loyalist Influence' on British Policy toward the United States after the American Revolution." *Eighteenth-Century Studies*, VII (1973), 1—17.

564 WHITAKER, Arthur P. *The Spanish-American Frontier: 1783—1795. The Westward Movement and the Spanish Retreat in the Mississippi Valley*. Boston, 1927.

565 WOOLERY, William K. "The Relation of Thomas Jefferson to American Foreign Policy, 1783—1793." *Johns Hopkins University Studies in Historical and Political Science*, XLV, No 2 (1927).

IV. The Federalist Era

1. General Studies

566 AMMON, Harry. "The Genet Mission and the Development of American Political Parties," *J Am Hist*, LII (1966), 725–741.

567 BARNBY, H. G. *The Prisoners of Algiers: An Account of the Forgotten American-Algerian War, 1785-1797*. New York, 1966.

568 BOWMAN, Albert H. "Jefferson, Hamilton and American Foreign Policy." *Pol Sci Q*, LXXI (1956), 18–41.

569 BOWMAN, Albert H. *The Struggle for Neutrality: Franco-American Diplomacy During the Federalist Era*. Knoxville, Tenn., 1974.

570 BURT, A. L. *The United States, Great Britain and British North America*. See **447**.

571 CHARLES, Jospeh. *The Origins of the American Party System*. New York, 1961.

572 COATSWORTH, John H. "American Trade with European Colonies in the Caribbean and South America, 1790–1812." *Wm and Mary Q*, XXIV (1967), 243–266.

573 GRABER, Doris A. *Public Opinion, the President and Foreign Policy: Four Case Studies from the Formative Years*. New York, 1968. Covers the years 1798 to 1823.

574 HAZEN, C. D. *Contemporary American Opinion of the French Revolution*. Baltimore, 1897.

575 HYNEMAN, Charles S. *The First American Neutrality: A Study of the American Understanding of Neutral Obligations during the Years 1792–1815*. Urbana, Ill., 1934.

576 LYCAN, Gilbert L. *Alexander Hamilton and American Foreign Policy: A Design for Greatness*. Norman, Okla., 1970.

577 McCOLLEY, Robert, ed. *Federalists, Republicans, and Foreign Entanglements, 1789–1815*. Englewood Cliffs, N.J., 1969.

578 MAYO, Bernard, ed. *Instructions to the British Ministers to the United States, 1791–1812*. Washington, 1941.

579 MILLER, John C. *Alexander Hamilton: Portrait in Paradox*. New York, 1959.

580 MILLER, John C. *The Federalist Era, 1789–1801*. New York, 1960.

581 SCHACHNER, Nathan. *The Founding Fathers*. New York, 1954.

582 SCHACHNER, Nathan. *Alexander Hamilton*. New York, 1945.

583 SELLEN, Robert W. "The American Museum, 1787–1792, as a Forum for Ideas of American Foreign Policy." *Pa Mag of Hist and Biog*, XCIII (1969), 179–189.

584 SOFAER, Abraham D. *War, Foreign Affairs and Constitutional Power: The Origins.* Cambridge, Mass., 1976.

585 TRESCOT, W. H. *The Diplomatic History of the Administrations of Washington and Adams, 1789—1801.* Boston, 1857.

586 WILLIAMS, William A. "The Age of Mercantilism: An Interpretation of the American Political Economy, 1763—1828." *Wm and Mary Q,* XV (1958), 419—437.

587 WOODBURY, Margaret. "Public Opinion in Philadelphia, 1789—1801." *Smith College Studies in History,* V (1919—1920), 5—138.

588 WRIGHT, Louis B. "The Founding Fathers and 'Splendid Isolation.' " *Hunt Lib Q,* VI (1943), 173—178.

2. The Washington Administration

589 AMMON, Harry. *The Genet Mission.* New York, 1973.*

590 BEMIS, Samuel Flagg. "The Background of Washington's Foreign Policy." *Yale Rev,* XVI (1927), 316—336.

591 BEMIS, Samuel Flagg. "John Quincy Adams and George Washington." *Proc Mass Hist Soc,* LXVII (1945), 365—384.

592 BEMIS, Samuel Flagg. "The United States and the Abortive Armed Neutrality of 1794." *Am Hist Rev,* XXIV (1918), 26—47.

593 BEMIS, Samuel Flagg. "Washington's Farewell Address: A Foreign Policy of Independence." *Am Hist Rev,* XXXIX (1934), 250—268.

594 BENTON, Elbert J. "The Spirit of Washington's Foreign Policy." *Review,* I (1910), 469—471.

595 BINNEY, Horace. *An Inquiry into the Formation of Washington's Farewell Address.* Philadelphia, 1859.

596 BOND, Beverley W., Jr. *The Monroe Mission to France, 1794—1796.* Baltimore, 1907.

597 CARROLL, John Alexander, and Mary Wells ASHWORTH. *First in Peace.* (Completes biography of George Washington by Douglas Southall Freeman.) New York, 1957.

598 CHARLES, Joseph. "Hamilton and Washington: The Origins of the American Party System." *Wm and Mary Q,* XII (1955), 217—267, 410—446, 581—630.

599 COBBETT, William. *A History of the American Jacobins, Commonly Denominated Democrats.* Philadelphia, 1796.

600 CROSS, Jack Lee. *London Mission: The First Critical Years.* East Lansing, Mich., 1968. The Pinckney mission to England in 1791.

601 DAVIS, Boothe Colwell. "The Myth of Washington's No Entangling Alliances." *University of Buffalo Studies,* IV (1923), 22—29.

602 DeCONDE, Alexander. *Entangling Alliance: Diplomacy and Politics under George Washington.* Durham, N.C., 1958.

603 DeCONDE, Alexander. "Washington's Farewell, the French Alliance, and the Election of 1796." *Miss Val Hist Rev*, XLIII (1957), 641—658.

604 FREEMAN, Douglas Southall. *George Washington, A Biography.* 7 vols. New York, 1948—1957.

605 HALLAM, Oscar. "Citizen Genet, His Contribution to International Law." *Am Law Rev*, LI (1917), 321—344.

606 HORSMAN, Reginald. "The British Indian Department and the Resistance to General Anthony Wayne, 1793—1795." *Miss Val Hist Rev*, XLIX (1962), 269—290.

607 JAMES, James Alton. "French Diplomacy and American Politics, 1794—1795." *Ann Rep Am Hist Assn for the Year 1911*, I (1913), 151—163.

608 LODGE, Henry Cabot. "Washington's Policies of Neutrality and National Defence." *War Addresses.* Boston, 1917.

609 MANNING, William Ray. "The Nootka Sound Controversy." *Ann Rep Am Hist Assn for the Year 1904* (1905), 279—478.

610 PALTSITS, Victor Hugo, ed. *Washington's Farewell Address.* New York, 1935.

611 PARTON, James. "The Exploits of Edmond Genet in the United States." *Atl Mon*, XXXI (1873), 385—405.

612 PETERSON, Merrill D. "Thomas Jefferson and Commercial Policy, 1783—1793." *Wm and Mary Q*, XXII (1965), 584—610.

613 RANDALL, James G. "George Washington and 'Entangling Alliances.' " *S Atl Q*, XXX (1931), 221—229.

614 SEARS, Louis Martin. *George Washington and the French Revolution.* Detroit, 1960.

615 SHACKELFORD, G. G. "William Short: Diplomat in Revolutionary France, 1785—1793." *Proc Am Philos Soc*, CII (1958), 596—612.

616 SMELSER, Marshall. "The Jacobin Phrenzy: Federalism and the Menace of Liberty, Equality, and Fraternity." *Rev Pol*, XIII (1951), 457—482.

617 SPENCER, Donald S. "Appeals to the People: The Later Genet Affair." *NY Hist Soc Q*, LIV (1970), 241—267.

618 THOMAS, Charles M. *American Neutrality in 1793: A Study in Cabinet Government.* New York, 1931.

619 USHER, Roland G. "Washington and Entangling Alliances." *N Am Rev*, CCIV (1916), 29—38.

620 WADSWORTH, James J. "Some Timely Advice from President Washington." *Sat Rev*, XLVIII (1968), 18, 97.

621 WARREN, Charles. *Jacobin and Junto.* Cambridge, Mass., 1931.

622 WEINBERG, Albert K. "Washington's 'Great Rule' in Its Historical Evolution." *Historiography and Urbanization: Essays in American History in Honor of W. Stull Holt.* Ed. Eric F. Goldman. Baltimore, 1941.

623 WRISTON, Henry M. "Washington and the Foundations of American Foreign Policy." *Minn Hist*, VIII (1927), 3—26.

3. The Jay and Pinckney Treaties

624 BEMIS, Samuel Flagg. *Jay's Treaty: A Study in Commerce and Diplomacy.* New Haven, Conn., 1962.

625 BEMIS, Samuel Flagg. "Jay's Treaty and the Northwest Boundary Gap." *Am Hist Rev*, XXVII (1922), 465 – 484.

626 BEMIS, Samuel Flagg. "The London Mission of Thomas Pinckney, 1792 – 1796." *Am Hist Rev*, XXVIII (1923), 228 – 247.

627 BEMIS, Samuel Flagg. *Pinckney's Treaty: America's Advantage from Europe's Distress, 1783 – 1800.* New Haven, Conn., 1962.

628 BOYD, Julian P. *Number 7: Alexander Hamilton's Secret Attempts to Control American Foreign Policy.* Princeton, N.J., 1964.

629 CHARLES, Joseph. "The Jay Treaty: The Origins of the American Party System." *Wm and Mary Q*, XII (1955), 581 – 630.

630 CHARLES, Joseph. *The Origins of the American Party System.* See **571.**

631 CLARFIELD, Gerard H. "Postscript to the Jay Treaty: Timothy Pickering and Anglo-American Relations, 1795 – 1797." *Wm and Mary Q*, XXIII (1966), 106 – 120.

632 CLARFIELD, Gerard H. "Victory in the West: A Study of the Role of Timothy Pickering in the Successful Consummation of Pinckney's Treaty." *Essex Inst Hist Coll*, CI (1965), 333 – 353.

633 COMBS, Jerald A. *The Jay Treaty: Political Battleground of the Founding Fathers.* Berkeley, Cal., 1969.

634 FARNHAM, Thomas J. "The Virginia Amendments of 1795: An Episode in the Opposition to Jay's Treaty." *Va Mag of Hist and Biog*, LXXV (1967), 75 – 88.

635 HAMMETT, Hugh B. "The Jay Treaty: Crisis Diplomacy in the New Nation." *Soc Stud*, LXV (1974), 10 – 17.

636 KRAMER, E. F., ed. "Senator Pierce Butler's Notes of the Debates on Jay's Treaty." *S Car Hist Mag*, LXII (1961), 1 – 9.

637 McCOWAN, G. S., Jr. "Chief Justice John Rutledge and the Jay Treaty." *S Car Hist Mag*, LXII (1961), 10 – 23.

638 OGG, Frederic Austin. "Jay's Treaty and the Slavery Interests of the United States." *Ann Rep Am Hist Assn for the Year 1901*, I (1902), 273 – 298.

639 PERKINS, Bradford, ed. "Lord Hawkesbury and the Jay-Grenville Negotations." *Miss Val Hist Rev*, XL (1953), 291 – 304.

640 STERLING, D. L. "A Federalist Opposes the Jay Treaty: The Letters of Samuel Bayard." *Wm and Mary Q*, XVIII (1961), 408 – 424.

641 WHITAKER, Arthur P. "Godoy's Knowledge of the Terms of Jay's Treaty." *Am Hist Rev*, XXXV (1930), 804 – 810.

642 WHITAKER, Arthur P. *The Spanish-American Frontier: 1783 – 1795.* See **564.**

643 WHITAKER, Arthur P. "New Light on the Treaty of San Lorenzo: An Essay in Historical Criticism." *Miss Val Hist Rev*, XV (1929), 435 – 454.

644 YOUNG, Raymond A. "Pinckney's Treaty—A New Perspective." *His Am Hist Rev*, XLIII (1963), 526—535.

645 ZAHNISER, Marvin R. "The First Pinckney Mission to France [1795]." *S Car Hist Mag*, LXVI (1965), 205—217.

4. The Adams Administration

646 ALLEN, G. W. *Our Naval War with France*. Boston, 1909.

647 BURRAGE, Henry S. "The St. Croix Commission, 1796—1798." *Me Hist Soc Coll*, VI (1895), 225—251.

648 CARR, James A. "John Adams and the Barbary Problem: The Myth and the Record." *Am Neptune*, XXVI (1966), 231—257.

649 CHINARD, Gilbert. *Honest John Adams*. Boston, 1933.

650 CLARFIELD, Gerard H. *Timothy Pickering and American Diplomacy, 1795—1800*. Columbia, Mo., 1969.

651 CROSBY, Alfred W., Jr. *America, Russia, Hemp, and Napoleon: American Trade with Russia and the Baltic, 1783—1812*. Columbus, Ohio, 1965.

652 DeCONDE, Alexander. "The Diplomacy of William Vans Murray." *Hunt Lib Q*, XV (1952), 185—194, 297—304.

653 DeCONDE, Alexander. "The Diplomacy of William Vans Murray." *Md Hist Mag*, XLVIII (1953), 1—26.

654 DeCONDE, Alexander. *The Quasi-War: The Politics and Diplomacy of the Undeclared War with France, 1797—1801*. New York, 1966.

655 HILL, Peter P. *William Vans Murray, Federalist Diplomat: The Shaping of Peace with France, 1797—1801*. Syracuse, N.Y., 1971.

656 JAMES, James Alton. "French Opinion as a Factor in Preventing War between France and the United States, 1795—1800." *Am Hist Rev*, XXX (1924), 44—55.

657 KRAMER, E. F. "Some New Light on the XYZ Affair: Elbridge Gerry's Reasons for Opposing War with France." *N Eng Q*, XXIX (1956), 509—513.

658 KURTZ, Stephen G. "The French Mission of 1799—1800: Concluding Chapter in the Statecraft of John Adams." *Pol Sci Q*, LXXX (1965), 543—577.

659 KURTZ, Stephen G. *The Presidency of John Adams*. Philadelphia, 1957.

660 LOKKE, Carl Ludwig. "The Trumbull Episode: A Prelude to the 'XYZ' Affair." *N Eng Q*, VII (1934), 100—114.

661 LYON, E. Wilson. "The Directory and the United States." *Am Hist Rev*, XLIII (1938), 514—532.

662 LYON, E. Wilson. "The Franco-American Convention of 1800." *J Mod Hist*, XII (1940), 305—333.

663 PERKINS, Bradford, ed. "A Diplomat's Wife in Philadelphia: Letters of Henrietta Liston, 1796—1800." *Wm and Mary Q*, XI (1954), 592—632.

664 PERKINS, Bradford. *The First Rapprochement: England and the United States, 1795–1805.* Philadelphia, 1955.

665 SMITH, Page. *John Adams.* 2 vols. New York, 1962.

666 STINCHCOMBE, William. "Talleyrand and the American Negotiations of 1797–1798." *J Am Hist,* LXII (1975), 575–590.

V. From Jefferson to Adams

1. General Studies

667 ADAMS, Charles Francis, ed. *Memoirs of John Quincy Adams.* 12 vols. Philadelphia, 1874–1877.

668 ADAMS, Henry. *History of the United States during the Administrations of Thomas Jefferson and James Madison.* 9 vols. New York, 1891–1896.

669 ADAMS, Henry. *The Life of Albert Gallatin.* Philadelphia, 1880.

670 AMMON, Harry. *James Monroe and the Quest for National Identity.* New York, 1971.

671 BEMIS, Samuel Flagg. *John Quincy Adams and the Foundations of American Foreign Policy.* New York, 1949.*

672 BENNS, F. L. *The American Struggle for the British West India Carrying Trade, 1815–1830.* Bloomington, Ind., 1923.

673 BERNSTEIN, Harry. *Origins of Inter-American Interest, 1700–1812.* Philadelphia, 1945.

674 BRANT, Irving. *James Madison: Secretary of State, 1801–1809.* Indianapolis, 1953.

675 BROWN, S. G., ed. *The Autobiography of James Monroe.* Syracuse, N.Y., 1959.

676 CROSBY, Alfred W., Jr. *America, Russia, Hemp, and Napoleon.* See **651.**

677 DANGERFIELD, George. *The Awakening of American Nationalism, 1815–1828.* New York, 1965.

678 DANGERFIELD, George. *The Era of Good Feelings.* New York, 1952.*

679 DUNNING, William A. *The British and the United States: A Review of Their Relations during the Century of Peace following the Treaty of Ghent.* New York, 1914.

680 EWING, Frank. *America's Forgotten Statesman: Albert Gallatin.* New York, 1959.

681 GOODWIN, Cardinal. *The Trans-Mississippi West, 1803–1853: A History of Its Acquisition and Settlement.* New York, 1922.

682 GRABER, Doris A. *Public Opinion, the President, and Foreign Policy.* See **573.**

683 LATANÉ, John H. "Jefferson's Influence on American Foreign Policy." *Alumni Bulletin, Univ. of Va.*, XVII (1924), 245–269.

684 LIPSKY, George A. *John Quincy Adams, His Theory and Ideas.* New York, 1950.

685 McLEMORE, Richard Aubrey. *Franco-American Diplomatic Relations, 1816–1836.* Baton Rouge, La., 1941.

686 MALONE, Dumas. *Jefferson the President: First Term, 1801–1805.* Boston, 1970.

687 MALONE, Dumas. *Jefferson the President: Second Term, 1805–1809.* Boston, 1974.

688 MARTIN, Thomas P. "Some International Aspects of the Antislavery Movement, 1818–1823." *J Econ and Bus Hist*, I (1928), 137–148.

689 MESICK, James. *The English Traveller in America 1785–1835.* New York, 1922.

690 PETERSON, Merrill D. *Thomas Jefferson and the New Nation.* New York, 1970.

691 PETERSON, Merrill D. "Henry Adams on Jefferson the President." *Va Q Rev*, XXXIX (1963), 187–201.

692 POWELL, J. H. *Richard Rush, Republican Diplomat, 1780–1859.* Philadelphia, 1942.

693 QUINCY, Josiah. *Memoir of the Life of John Quincy Adams.* Boston, 1859.

694 SEARS, Louis Martin. "Jefferson and the Law of Nations." *Am Pol Sci Rev*, XIII (1919), 379–399.

695 SHULIM, J. I. "The United States Views Russia in the Napoleonic Age." *Proc Am Philos Soc*, CII (1958), 148–159.

696 THISTLETHWAITE, Frank. *The Anglo-American Connection in the Early Nineteenth Century.* Philadelphia, 1959.

697 WALTERS, Raymond, Jr. *Albert Gallatin: Jeffersonian Financier and Diplomat.* New York, 1957.

698 WEBSTER, C. K. *The Foreign Policy of Castlereagh, 1812–1822.* 2 vols. London, 1934.

699 WHITE, Leonard. *The Jeffersonians: A Study in Administrative History, 1801–1829.* New York, 1951.

700 WILLSON, Beckles. *America's Ambassadors to England, 1785–1929: A Narrative of Anglo-American Diplomatic Relations.* New York, 1929.

701 WILLSON, Beckles. *Friendly Relations: A Narrative of Britain's Ministers and Ambassadors to America, 1791–1930.* Boston, 1934.

702 WILTSE, Charles M. *John C. Calhoun, Nationalist, 1782–1828.* Indianapolis, 1944.

703 WOODRESS, James. *A Yankee's Odyssey: The Life of Joel Barlow.* Philadelphia, 1958.

2. Louisiana, West Florida, the West Indies, and North Africa

704 ADAMS, Mary P. "Jefferson's Reaction to the Treaty of San Ildefonso." *J S Hist*, XXI (1955), 173–188.

705 ALLEN, G. W. *Our Navy and the Barbary Corsairs*. Boston, 1905.

706 BAILEY, H. C., and B. C. WEBER. "A British Reaction to the Treaty of San Ildefonso." *Wm and Mary Q*, XVII (1960), 242–246.

707 BARBE-MARBOIS, Marquis de. *History of Louisiana*. Philadelphia, 1830.

708 BIXLER, R. W. *The Open Door on the Old Barbary Coast*. New York, 1959.

709 BRADLEY, Jared W. "W. C. C. Claiborne and Spain: Foreign Affairs under Jefferson and Madison, 1801–1811." *La Hist*, XII (1971), 297–314; XIII (1972), 5–26.

710 BROOKS, Philip C. "Spain's Farewell to Louisiana, 1803–1821." *Miss Val Hist Rev*, XXVII (1940), 29–42.

711 CANTOR, Milton, ed. "A Connecticut Yankee in a Barbary Court: Joel Barlow's Algerian Letters to His Wife." *Wm and Mary Q*, XIX (1962), 172–194.

712 CANTOR, Milton. "Joel Barlow's Mission to Algiers." *The Historian*, XXV (1963), 172–194.

713 COX, Isaac J. *The Louisiana-Texas Frontier*. 2 vols. Austin, Tex., 1902–1913.

714 COX, Isaac J. "The Significance of the Louisiana-Texas Frontier." *Proc Miss Val Hist Assn*, III (1911), 198–213.

715 COX, Isaac J. "The American Intervention in West Florida." *Am Hist Rev*, XVII (1912), 290–311.

716 COX, Isaac J. "General Wilkinson and His Later Intrigues with the Spaniards." *Am Hist Rev*, XIX (1914), 794–812.

717 COX, Isaac J. *The West Florida Controversy, 1798–1813: A Study in American Diplomacy*. Baltimore, 1918.

718 EGAN, Clifford L. "The United States, France, and West Florida, 1803–1807." *Fla Hist Q*, XLVII (1969), 227–252.

719 FARRAND, Max. "The Commercial Privileges of the Treaty of 1803." *Am Hist Rev*, VII (1902), 494–499.

720 IRWIN, Ray W. *The Diplomatic Relations of the United States with the Barbary Powers, 1776–1816*. See **553**.

721 KNUDSON, Jerry W. "Newspaper Reaction to the Louisiana Purchase: 'This New, Immense, Unbounded World.' " *Mo Hist Rev*, LXIII (1969), 182–213.

722 LOKKE, Carl Ludwig. "Jefferson and the Leclerc Expedition." *Am Hist Rev*, XXXIII (1928), 322–328.

723 LONGFORD, N. P. "The Louisiana Purchase and Preceding Spanish Intrigues for Dismemberment of the Union." *Minn Hist Soc Coll*, IX (1901), 453–508.

724 LYON, E. Wilson. *Louisiana in French Diplomacy, 1759–1804*. Norman, Okla., 1934.

725 MARKS, Henry S., ed. "Boundary Disputes in the Republic of West Florida in 1810." *La Hist*, XII (1971), 355–365.

726 OGG, Frederic Austin, and Dunbar ROWLAND. "The American Intervention in West Florida." *Proc Miss Val Hist Assn*, IV (1912), 47–58.

727 PELZER, Louis. "Economic Factors in the Acquisition of Louisiana." *Proc Miss Val Hist Assn*, V (1913), 109–128.

728 PERKINS, Bradford. "England and the Louisiana Question." *Hunt Lib Q*, XVIII (1955), 279–295.

729 RANDALL, E. O. "The Louisiana Purchase." *Ohio St Arch and Hist Q*, XIII (1904), 248–262.

730 ROWLAND, Dunbar. "Mississippi in the Transfer of the Louisiana Purchase by France to the United States." *La Hist Q*, XIII (1930), 235–245.

731 SKOLNIK, Richard. *1803: Jefferson's Decision, the United States Purchases Louisiana*. New York, 1969.

732 SLOANE, W. M. "The World Aspects of the Louisiana Purchase." *Am Hist Rev*, IX (1904), 507–521.

733 SPARKS, Jared. "The History of the Louisiana Treaty." *N Am Rev*, XXVIII (1829), 389–418.

734 SPRAGUE, Stuart S. "Jefferson, Kentucky and the Closing of the Port of New Orleans, 1802–1803." *Register of the Kentucky Historical Society*, LXX (1972), 312–317.

735 STODDARD, Theodore Lothrop. *The French Revolution in San Domingo*. New York, 1914.

736 TURNER, Frederick Jackson. "The Diplomatic Contest for the Mississippi Valley." *Atl Mon*, XCIII (1904), 676–691, 807–817.

737 WHITAKER, Arthur P. "France and the American Deposit at New Orleans." *His Am Hist Rev*, XI (1931), 485–502.

738 WHITAKER, Arthur P. *The Mississippi Question 1795–1803*. New York, 1934.

739 WHITAKER, Arthur P. "The Retrocession of Louisiana in Spanish Policy." *Am Hist Rev*, XXXIX (1934), 454–476.

740 WRIGHT, Louis B., and Julia H. MACLEOD. *The First Americans in North Africa: William Eaton's Struggle for a Vigorous Policy against the Barbary Pirates, 1799–1805*. Princeton, N.J., 1945.

741 WRIGHT, M. J. "Some Account of the Transfer of the Territory of Louisiana from France to the United States." *Pub S Hist Assn*, II (1898), 17–28.

3. Embargo and the War of 1812

742 ANDERSON, Dice R. "The Insurgents of 1811." *Ann Rep Am Hist Assn for the Year 1911,* I (1913), 167–176.

743 BARLOW, William R. "Ohio's Congressmen and the War of 1812." *Ohio Hist,* LXXII (1963), 175–194.

744 BEIRNE, F. F. *The War of 1812.* New York, 1949.

745 BRANT, Irving. *James Madison: Commander in Chief.* Indianapolis, 1961.

746 BRANT, Irving. *James Madison: The President, 1809–1812.* Indianapolis, 1956.

747 BRANT, Irving. "Joel Barlow, Madison's Stubborn Minister." *Wm and Mary Q,* XV (1958), 438–451.

748 BRANT, Irving. "Madison and the War of 1812." *Va Mag of Hist and Biog,* LXXIV (1966), 51–67.

749 BROWN, Roger H. *The Republic in Peril: 1812.* New York, 1971.

750 BROWN, Roger H., Alexander DeCONDE, Reginald HORSMAN, and Norman K. RISJORD. "The War Hawks and the War of 1812." *Ind Mag of Hist,* LX (1964), 119–158. Four essays on the theme.

751 BROWN, Wilburt S. *The Amphibious Campaign for West Florida and Louisiana, 1814–1815: A Critical Review of Strategy and Tactics at New Orleans.* University, Ala., 1969.

752 BURT, A. L. *The United States, Great Britain and British North America.* See **447.**

753 CADY, J. F. "Western Opinion and the War of 1812." *Ohio St Arch and Hist Q,* XXXIII (1924), 427–476.

754 CARR, Albert Z. *The Coming of War: An Account of the Remarkable Events Leading to the War of 1812.* Garden City, N.Y., 1960.

755 CLAUDER, Anna C. *American Commerce as Affected by the Wars of the French Revolution and Napoleon, 1793–1812.* Philadelphia, 1932.

756 COLEMAN, Christopher B. "The Ohio Valley in the Preliminaries of the War of 1812." *Miss Val Hist Rev,* VII (1920), 39–50.

757 COLES, Harry L. *The War of 1812.* Chicago, 1965.

758 EGAN, Clifford L. "The Origins of the War of 1812: Three Decades of Historical Writing." *Mil Affairs,* XXXVIII (1974), 72–75.

759 ENGLEMAN, F. L. *The Peace of Christmas Eve.* New York, 1962.

760 FORD, Worthington C. "The Treaty of Ghent, and After." *Proc Wis Hist Soc,* LXII (1915), 78–106.

761 GATES, Charles M. "The West in American Diplomacy, 1812–1815." *Miss Val Hist Rev,* XXVI (1940), 499–510.

762 GLOVER, Richard. "The French Fleet, 1807–1814: Britain's Problem and Madison's Opportunity." *J Mod Hist*, XXXIX (1967), 233–252.

763 GOLDER, Frank A. "The Russian Offer of Mediation in the War of 1812." *Pol Sci Q*, XXXI (1916), 380–391.

764 GOODMAN, Warren H. "The Origins of the War of 1812: A Survey of Changing Interpretations." *Miss Val Hist Rev*, XXVIII (1941), 171–186.

765 HACKER, Louis M. "Western Land Hunger and the War of 1812." *Miss Val Hist Rev*, X (1924), 365–395.

766 HATZENBUEHLER, Ronald L. "Party Unity and the Decision for War in the House of Representatives, 1812." *Wm and Mary Q*, XXIX (1972), 367–390.

767 HECKSCHER, Eli F. *The Continental System*. Oxford, Eng., 1922.

768 HILL, F. T. "The Treaty of Ghent." *Atl Mon*, CXIV (1914), 231–241.

769 HITSMAN, J. M. *The Incredible War of 1812*. Toronto, Can., 1965.

770 HORSMAN, Reginald. "British Indian Policy in the Northwest, 1807–1812." *Miss Val Hist Rev*, XLV (1958), 51–66.

771 HORSMAN, Reginald. *The Causes of the War of 1812*. Philadelphia, 1962.

772 HORSMAN, Reginald. *The War of 1812*. New York, 1969.

773 HORSMAN, Reginald. "Western War Aims, 1811–1812." *Ind Mag of Hist*, LIII (1957), 1–18.

774 JONES, Wilbur D. "A British View of the War of 1812 and the Peace Negotiations." *Miss Val Hist Rev*, XLV (1958), 481–487.

775 KAPLAN, Lawrence S. "France and Madison's Decision for War, 1812." *Miss Val Hist Rev*, L (1964), 652–671.

776 KAPLAN, Lawrence S. "France and the War of 1812." *J Am Hist*, LVII (1970), 36–47.

777 KAPLAN, Lawrence S. "Jefferson, the Napoleonic Wars, and the Balance of Power." *Wm and Mary Q*, XIV (1957), 196–217.

778 KAPLAN, Lawrence S. "Jefferson's Foreign Policy and Napoleon's Ideologues." *Wm and Mary Q*, XIX (1962), 344–359.

779 LATIMER, Margaret K. "South Carolina—A Protagonist of the War of 1812." *Am Hist Rev*, LXI (1956), 914–929.

780 LEMMON, Sarah McCulloh. *Frustrated Patriots: North Carolina in the War of 1812*. Chapel Hill, N.C., 1973.

781 LEWIS, Howard T. "A Re-analysis of the Causes of the War of 1812." *Americana*, VI (1911), 506–516, 577–585.

782 LUCAS, Sir Charles P. *The Canadian War of 1812*. Oxford, Eng., 1906.

783 MAHAN, Alfred Thayer. *Sea Power in Its Relations to the War of 1812*. 2 vols. Boston, 1905.

784 MASON, Philip P. *After Tippecanoe: Some Aspects of the War of 1812*. East Lansing, Mich., 1963.

785 MILLETT, Stephen M. "Bellicose Nationalism in Ohio: The Origin of the War of 1812." *Canadian Review of Studies of Nationalism*, I (1974), 221–240.

786 MORISON, Samuel Eliot. "Our Most Unpopular War, 1812–1815." *Proc Mass Hist Soc*, LXXX (1968), 38–54.

787 OWSLEY, Frank Lawrence, Jr. "The Role of the South in the British Grand Strategy in the War of 1812." *Tenn Hist Q*, XXXI (1972), 22–38.

788 PANCAKE, J. S. "The 'oInvisibles': A Chapter in the Opposition to President Madison." *J S Hist*, XXI (1955), 17–37.

789 PERKINS, Bradford. *Castlereagh and Adams: England and the United States, 1812–1823*. Berkeley, Cal., 1964.

790 PERKINS, Bradford. "George Canning, Great Britain, and the United States, 1807–1809." *Am Hist Rev*, LXIII (1957), 1–22.

791 PERKINS, Bradford. "George Joy, American Propagandist at London, 1805–1815." *N Eng Q*, XXXIV (1961), 191–210.

792 PERKINS, Bradford. *Prologue to War: England and the United States, 1805–1812*. Berkeley, Cal., 1961.

793 PRATT, Julius W. *Expansionists of 1812*. New York, 1925.

794 PRATT, Julius W. "Fur Trade Strategy and the American Left Flank in the War of 1812." *Am Hist Rev*, XL (1935), 246–273.

795 PRATT, Julius W. "Western Aims in the War of 1812." *Miss Val Hist Rev*, XII (1925), 36–50.

796 RICHMOND, A. A. "Napoleon and the Armed Neutrality of 1800: A Diplomatic Challenge to British Sea Power." *J Royal United Service Institution*, CIV (1959), 186–194.

797 RISJORD, Norman K. "1812: Conservatives, War Hawks, and the Nation's Honor." *Wm and Mary Q*, XVIII (1961), 196–210.

798 RUTLAND, Robert A. *Madison's Alternatives: The Jeffersonian Republicans and the Coming of War, 1805–1812*. Philadelphia, 1975.

799 SAPIO, Victor A. "Expansion and Economic Depression as Factors in Pennsylvania's Support of the War of 1812: An Application of the Pratt and Taylor Theses to the Keystone State." *Pa Hist*, XXXV (1968), 379–405.

800 SAPIO, Victor A. *Pennsylvania and the War of 1812*. Lexington, Ky., 1970.

801 SEARS, A. B. *Thomas Worthington*. Columbus, Ohio, 1958.

802 SEARS, Louis Martin. *Jefferson and the Embargo*. Durham, N.C., 1927.

803 SMITH, Abbot. "Mr. Madison's War: An Unsuccessful Experiment in the Conduct of National Policy." *Pol Sci Q*, LVII (1942), 229–246.

804 SPIVAK, Burton. "Jefferson, England, and the Embargo: Trading Wealth and Republican Value in the Shaping of American Diplomacy, 1804–1809." Doctoral dissertation, University of Virginia, 1975.

805 STEEL, Anthony. "Impressment in the Monroe-Pinckney Negotiation, 1806–1807." *Am Hist Rev*, LVII (1952), 352–369.

806 STEEL, Anthony. "More Light on the Chesapeake." *Mariner's Mirror*, XXXIX (1953), 243–265.

807 TAYLOR, George R. "Agrarian Discontent in the Mississippi Valley Preceding the War of 1812." *J Pol Econ*, XXXIX (1931), 471–505.

808 TAYLOR, George R. "Prices in the Mississippi Valley Preceding the War of 1812." *J Econ and Bus Hist*, III (1930), 148–163.

809 UPDYKE, F. A. *The Diplomacy of the War of 1812*. Baltimore, 1915.

810 WARE, M. F. "A Sidelight on the War of 1812." *Hist Teach Mag*, V (1914), 319—323.

811 WEHTJE, Myron F. "Opposition in Virginia to the War of 1812." *Va Mag of Hist and Biog*, LXXVIII (1970), 65—86.

812 WHITE, Patrick C. T. *A Nation on Trial: America and the War of 1812*. New York, 1965.

813 WILTSE, Charles M. "The Authorship of the War Report of 1812." *Am Hist Rev*, XLIX (1944), 253—259.

814 ZASLOW, Morris, ed. *The Defended Border: Upper Canada and the War of 1812*. Toronto, 1964.

815 ZIMMERMAN, James F. *Impressment of American Seamen*. See **111**.

4. East Florida, Latin America, and Early Pan Americanism

816 AUCHMUTY, James J. *The United States Government and Latin American Independence, 1810— 1830*. London, 1937.

817 BAKER, Maury D., Jr. "The United States and Piracy: The Latin American Wars of Independence." Doctoral dissertation, Duke University, 1946.

818 BAKER, Maury. "The Spanish War Scare of 1816." *Mid-America*, XLV (1963), 67—78.

819 BEMIS, Samuel Flagg. *Early Diplomatic Missions from Buenos Aires to the United States, 1811— 1824*. Worcestor, Mass., 1940.

820 BILLINGSLEY, Edward B. *In Defense of Neutral Rights: The United States Navy and the Wars of Independence in Chile and Peru*. Chapel Hill, N.C., 1967.

821 BROOKS, Philip C. *Diplomacy and the Borderlands: The Adams-Onis Treaty of 1819*. Berkeley, Cal., 1939.

822 BROOKS, Philip C. "The Pacific Coast's First International Boundary Delineation, 1816-1819." *Pac Hist Rev*, III (1934), 62—79.

823 CLEVEN, N. Andrew N. *The First Panama Mission and the Congress of the United States*. n.p., 1928.

824 COX, Isaac J. "Monroe and the Early Mexican Revolutionary Agents." *Ann Rep Am Hist Assn for the Year 1911*, I (1913), 197—215.

825 COX, Isaac J. "The Pan-American Policy of Jefferson and Wilkinson." *Miss Val Hist Rev*, I (1914), 212—239.

826 CRAINE, Eugene R. *The United States and the Independence of Buenos Aires*. Hays, Kans., 1961.

827 FISHER, Lillian E. "American Influence upon the Movement for Mexican Independence." *Miss Val Hist Rev*, XIII (1932), 463—478.

828 FULLER, H. B. *The Purchase of Florida: Its History and Diplomacy.* Cleveland, 1906.

829 GRAEBNER, Norman A. "United States Gulf Commerce with Mexico, 1822—1848." *Inter-American Economic Affairs*, V (1951), 36—51.

830 GRIFFIN, Charles C. *The United States and the Disruption of the Spanish Empire, 1810— 1822: A Study of the Relations of the United States with Spain and with the Rebel Spanish Colonies.* New York, 1937.

831 HOSKINS, H. L. "The Hispanic American Policy of Henry Clay, 1816—1828." *His Am Hist Rev*, VII (1927), 460—478.

832 JAMES, Marquis. *Andrew Jackson, The Border Captain.* Indianapolis, 1933.

833 JOHNSON, J. J. "Early Relations of the United States with Chile." *Pac Hist Rev*, XIII (1944), 260—270.

834 LOCKEY, J. B. *Pan-Americanism: Its Beginnings.* New York, 1920.

835 MONEY, H. D. "The United States and Spanish-American Colonies: A Reply." *N Am Rev*, CLXV (1897), 356—363.

836 MOORE, John Bassett. "Henry Clay and Pan-Americanism." *Columbia Uni Q*, XVII (1915), 346—362.

837 NEUMANN, William L. "United States Aid to the Chilean Wars of Independence." *His Am Hist Rev*, XXVII (1947), 204—219.

838 PAXSON, F. L. *The Independence of the South American Republics: A Study in Recognition and Foreign Policy.* Philadelphia, 1903.

839 PRATT, Edwin J. "Anglo-American Commercial and Political Rivalry on the Plata, 1820—1830." *His Am Hist Rev*, XI (1931), 302—335.

840 REINHOLD, F. L. "New Research on the First Pan-American Congress Held at Panama in 1826." *His Am Hist Rev*, XVIII (1938), 342—363.

841 RIPPY, J. Fred. *Rivalry of the United States and Great Britain over Latin America, 1808— 1830.* Baltimore, 1929.

842 ROBERTSON, William Spence. "The First Legations of the United States in Latin America." *Miss Val Hist Rev*, II (1915), 183—212.

843 ROBERTSON, William Spence. *France and Latin American Independence.* Baltimore, 1939.

844 ROBERTSON, William Spence. "The Recognition of the Hispanic American Nations by the United States." *His Am Hist Rev*, I (1918), 239—269.

845 ROBERTSON, William Spence. "The United States and Spain in 1822." *Am Hist Rev*, XX (1915), 781—800.

846 ROBERTSON, William Spence. "Russia and the Emancipation of Spanish America." *His Am Hist Rev*, XXI (1941), 196—221.

847 ROMERO, Matías. "The United States and the Liberation of the Spanish-American Colonies." *N Am Rev*, CLXV (1897), 70—86.

848 SHEPHERD, W. R. "Bolivar and the United States." *His Am Hist Rev*, I (1918), 270—298.

849 STEWART, Watt. "The South American Commission, 1817—1818." *His Am Hist Rev*, IX (1929), 31—59.

850 STEWART, Watt. "The United States—Argentina Commercial Negotiations of 1825." *His Am Hist Rev*, XIII (1933), 367—379.

851 WEBER, Ralph E. "Joel R. Poinsett's Secret Mexican Dispatch Twenty." *S Car Hist Mag*, LXXV (1974), 67 – 76.

852 WEBSTER, C. K., ed. *Britain and the Independence of Latin America, 1812 – 1830.* 2 vols. London, 1938.

853 WHITAKER, Arthur P. *The United States and the Independence of Latin America, 1800 – 1830.* Baltimore, 1941.

854 WILLIAMS, Mary W. *Anglo-American Isthmian Diplomacy, 1815 – 1915.* Washington, 1916.

855 WYLLYS, Rufus Kay. "The East Florida Revolution of 1812 – 1814." *His Am Hist Rev*, IX (1929), 415 – 445.

5. The Monroe Doctrine

856 BORNHOLDT, Laura. "The Abbé de Pradt and the Monroe Doctrine." *His Am Hist Rev*, XXIV (1944), 201 – 221.

857 BRANCO, Baron Rio. *Brazil, the United States and the Monroe Doctrine.* Washington, 1908.

858 CHANDLER, Charles Lyons. "United States Commerce with Latin America at the Promulgation of the Monroe Doctrine." *Q J Econ*, XXXVIII (1924), 466 – 487.

859 CLINE, Myrtle A. *American Attitude toward the Greek War of Independence, 1821 – 1828.* Atlanta, Ga., 1930.

860 CRAVEN, Wesley Frank, Jr. "The Risk of the Monroe Doctrine, 1823 – 1824." *His Am Hist Rev*, VII (1927), 320 – 333.

861 CRESSON, W. P. *The Holy Alliance: The European Background of the Monroe Doctrine.* New York, 1922.

862 DAKIN, Douglas. *The Greek Struggle for Independence, 1821 – 1833.* Berkeley, Cal., 1973.

863 DAVIS, T. B., Jr. "Carlos De Alvear and James Monroe: New Light on the Origin of the Monroe Doctrine." *His Am Hist Rev*, XXIII (1943), 632 – 649.

864 EARLE, Edward M. "American Interest in the Greek Cause, 1821 – 1827." *Am Hist Rev*, XXXIII (1927), 44 – 63.

865 FORD, Worthington C. "John Quincy Adams and the Monroe Doctrine." *Am Hist Rev*, VII (1902), 676 – 696.

866 HART, Albert Bushnell. *The Monroe Doctrine: An Interpretation.* Boston, 1916.

867 LAWSON, L. A. *The Relation of British Policy to the Declaration of the Monroe Doctrine.* New York, 1922.

868 LOGAN, John A. *No Transfer.* See **217**.

869 MacCORKLE, William A. *The Personal Genesis of the Monroe Doctrine.* New York, 1923.

870 McGEE, Gale W. "The Monroe Doctrine – A Stopgap Measure." *Miss Val Hist Rev*, XXXVII (1951), 233 – 250.

871 MAY, Ernest R. *The Making of the Monroe Doctrine.* Cambridge, Mass., 1975.

872 MAZOUR, Anatole G. "The Russian-American and Anglo-Russian Conventions, 1824—1825: An Interpretation." *Pac Hist Rev,* XIV (1945), 303—310.

873 MAZOUR, Anatole G. "The Prelude to Russia's Departure from America." *Pac Hist Rev,* X (1941), 311—319.

874 MORISON, Samuel Eliot. "The Origin of the Monroe Doctrine, 1775—1823." *Economica,* IV (1924), 27—51.

875 NERVAL, Gaston. *Autopsy of the Monroe Doctrine.* New York, 1934.

876 NICHOLS, Irby C., Jr. "The Russian Ukase and the Monroe Doctrine: A Reevaluation." *Pac Hist Rev,* XXXVI (1967), 13—26.

877 PERKINS, Bradford. "The Suppressed Dispatch of H. U. Addington, Washington, November 3, 1823." *His Am Hist Rev,* XXXVII (1957), 480—485.

878 PERKINS, Bradford. *Castlereagh and Adams: England and the United States, 1812—1823.* See **789**.

879 PERKINS, Dexter. *The Monroe Doctrine, 1823—1826.* Cambridge, Mass., 1927.

880 REDDAWAY, W. F. *The Monroe Doctrine.* Cambridge, Eng., 1898.

881 ROBERTSON, William Spence. "The Monroe Doctrine Abroad in 1823—1824." *Am Pol Sci Rev,* VI (1912), 546—563.

882 ROBERTSON, William Spence. "South America and the Monroe Doctrine, 1824—1828." *Pol Sci Q,* XXX (1915), 82—105.

883 RUSH, Richard. *A Residence at the Court of London.* London, 1833.

884 SCHELLENBERG, T. R. "Jeffersonian Origins of the Monroe Doctrine." *His Am Hist Rev,* XIV (1934), 1—32.

885 STEWART, Watt. "Argentina and the Monroe Doctrine, 1824—1828." *His Am Hist Rev,* X (1930), 26—32.

886 TATUM, Edward H., Jr. *The United States and Europe, 1815—1823: A Study in the Background of the Monroe Doctrine.* Berkeley, Cal., 1936.

887 TEMPERLEY, Harold W. V. "The Later American Policy of George Canning." *Am Hist Rev,* XI (1906), 779—797.

VI. An Era of General Peace: 1830-1860

1. General Studies

888 ADAMS, Ephraim Douglas. "The British Traveler in America." *Pol Sci Q,* XXIX (1914), 244—264.

889 CHITWOOD, Oliver P. *John Tyler: Champion of the Old South*. New York, 1939.

890 CURRENT, Richard N. *Daniel Webster and the Rise of National Conservatism*. Boston, 1955.

891 CURTIS, G. T. *Life of James Buchanan*. 2 vols. New York, 1883.

892 CURTIS, G. T. *Life of Daniel Webster*. 2 vols. New York, 1889.

893 CURTIS, James C. *The Fox at Bay: Martin Van Buren and the Presidency, 1837—1841*. Lexington, Ky., 1970.

894 DUCKETT, Alvin L. *John Forsyth, Political Tactician*. Athens, Ga., 1962.

895 FUESS, Claude M. *Daniel Webster*. 2 vols. Boston, 1930.

896 GIBSON, F. E. *The Attitudes of the New York Irish toward State and National Affairs, 1848—1892*. New York, 1951.

897 KLEIN, Philip S. *President James Buchanan*. University Park, Pa., 1962.

898 McCORMAC, Eugene Irving. *James K. Polk: A Political Biography*. Berkeley, Cal., 1922.

899 NEVINS, Allan, ed. *Polk, the Diary of a President, 1845—1849*. New York, 1966.

900 NEVINS, Allan, ed. *The Diary of Philip Hone, 1828—1851*. New York, 1936.

901 NICHOLS, Roy F. *Franklin Pierce*. Philadelphia, 1931.

902 OESTE, George Irwin. *John Randolph Clay, America's First Career Diplomat*. Philadelphia, 1966.

903 QUAIFE, Milo Milton, ed. *The Diary of James K. Polk during His Presidency, 1845—1849*. 4 vols. Chicago, 1910.

904 REEVES, Jesse S. *American Diplomacy under Tyler and Polk*. Baltimore, 1907.

905 SHEWMAKER, Kenneth E. "Daniel Webster and the Politics of Foreign Policy, 1850—1852." *J Am Hist*, LXIII (1976), 303—315.

906 SPENCER, Ivor D. *The Victor and the Spoils: A Life of William L. Marcy*. Providence, R.I., 1959.

907 STACEY, C. P. "The Myth of the Unguarded Frontier, 1815—1871." *Am Hist Rev*, LVI (1950), 1—18.

908 TUCKERMAN, Bayard, ed. *The Diary of Philip Hone, 1828—1851*. 2 vols. New York, 1889.

909 WAYLAND, Francis Fry. *Andrew Stevenson, Democrat and Diplomat, 1785—1857*. Philadelphia, 1949.

2. Great Britain and Canada

910 ADAMS, Ephraim Douglas. "Lord Ashburton and the Treaty of Washington." *Am Hist Rev*, XVII (1912), 764—782.

911 ASHLEY, Evelyn. *Life of Henry John Temple, Viscount Palmerston, with Selections from his Diaries and Correspondence.* 3 vols. London, 1870 – 1874.

912 BERGER, Max. *The British Traveller in America, 1836 – 1860.* New York, 1943.

913 BONHAM, Milledge Louis, Jr. "Alexander McLeod: Bone of Contention." *New York Hist,* XVIII (1937), 189 – 217.

914 BOURNE, Kenneth. *Britain and the Balance of Power in North America, 1815 – 1908.* See **113**.

915 BREBNER, John Bartlet. "Joseph Howe and the Crimean Enlistment Controversy between Great Britain and the United States." *Can Hist Rev,* XI (1930), 300 – 327.

916 BRIGHTFIELD, M. F. "America and the Americans, 1840 – 1860, as Depicted in English Novels of the Period." *Am Lit,* XXXI (1959), 309 – 324.

917 BURRAGE, Henry S. "The American Attitude of Maine in the Northeastern Boundary Controversy." *Me Hist Soc Coll,* I (1904), 353 – 368.

918 BURRAGE, Henry S. *Maine in the Northeastern Boundary Dispute.* Portland, Maine, 1919.

919 CALLAHAN, James M. *American Foreign Policy in Canadian Relations.* New York, 1937.

920 CORBETT, Percy E. *The Settlement of Canadian-American Disputes: A Critical Study of Methods and Results.* New Haven, Conn., 1937.

921 COREY, Albert B. *The Crisis of 1830 – 1842 in Canadian-American Relations.* New Haven, Conn., 1941.

922 CURRENT, Richard N. "Webster's Propaganda and the Ashburton Treaty." *Miss Val Hist Rev,* XXXIV (1947), 187 – 200.

923 DYKSTRA, David Laurie. "The United States and Great Britain and the Shift in the Balance of Power on the North American Continent, 1837 – 1848." Doctoral dissertation, University of Virginia, 1973.

924 GASH, Norman. *Politics in the Age of Peel, 1830 – 1850.* London, 1953.

925 GILL, George J. "Edward Everett and the Northeastern Boundary Controversy." *N Eng Q,* XLII (1969), 201 – 213.

926 GORDON, H. T. *The Treaty of Washington, Concluded August 9, 1842, by Daniel Webster and Lord Ashburton.* Berkeley, Cal., 1908.

927 GOUGH, Barry M. "British Policy in the San Juan Boundary Dispute, 1854 – 72." *Pac Northwest Q,* LXII (1971), 59 – 68.

928 GUILLET, Edwin Clarence. *The Lives and Times of the Patriots: An Account of the Rebellion in Upper Canada, 1837 – 1838, and of the Patriot Agitation in the United States, 1837 – 1842.* Toronto, Can., 1968.

929 HAYNES, Frederick Emory. *The Reciprocity Treaty with Canada of 1854.* Baltimore, 1892.

930 HECHT, Irene W. D. "Israel D. Andrews and the Reciprocity Treaty of 1854: A Reappraisal." *Can Hist Rev,* XLIV (1963), 313 – 329.

931 HIDY, Ralph Willard. *The House of Baring in American Trade and Finance: English Merchant Bankers at Work, 1763 – 1861.* Cambridge, Mass., 1949.

932 HODGINS, Thomas Q. C. *British and American Diplomacy Affecting Canada.* Toronto, Can., 1900.

933 JONES, Howard. "The *Caroline* Affair." *The Historian*, XXXVIII (1976), 485—502.

934 JONES, Wilbur D. *The American Problem in British Diplomacy, 1841—1861.* Athens, Ga., 1973.

935 JONES, Wilbur D. "The Influence of Slavery on the Webster-Ashburton Negotiations." *J S Hist*, XXII (1956), 48—58.

936 JONES, Wilbur D. *Lord Aberdeen and the Americas.* Athens, Ga., 1958.

937 JONES, Wilbur D. "Lord Ashburton and the Maine Boundary Negotiations." *Miss Val Hist Rev*, XL (1953), 477—490.

938 KNAPLUND, Paul. "The Armaments on the Great Lakes, 1844." *Am Hist Rev*, XL (1935), 473—476.

939 LANDRY, H. E. "Slavery and the Slave Trade in Atlantic Diplomacy, 1850—1861." *J S Hist*, XXVII (1961), 184—207.

940 LeDUC, Thomas. "The Maine Frontier and the Northeastern Boundary Controversy." *Am Hist Rev*, LIII (1947), 30—41.

941 LeDUC, Thomas. "The Webster-Ashburton Treaty and the Minnesota Iron Ranges." *J Am Hist*, LI (1964), 476—481.

942 LONG, J. W., Jr. "The Origin and Development of the San Juan Island Boundary Controversy." *Pac Northwest Q*, XLIII (1952), 187—213.

943 LOWENTHAL, David. "The Maine Press and the Aroostook War." *Can Hist Rev*, XXXII (1951), 315—336.

944 MILLER, David Hunter. *San Juan Archipelago: Study of the Joint Occupation of San Juan Island.* Bellows Falls, Vt., 1943.

945 MOORE, D. R. *Canada and the United States, 1815—1830.* Chicago, 1910.

946 OFFICER, Lawrence H., and Lawrence B. SMITH. "The Canadian-American Reciprocity Treaty of 1855 to 1866." *J Econ Hist*, XXVIII (1968), 598—623.

947 OVERMAN, W. D. "I. D. Andrews and Reciprocity in 1854: An Episode in Dollar Diplomacy." *Can Hist Rev*, XV (1934), 248—263.

948 PARKER, Charles Stuart, ed. *Sir Robert Peel.* 3 vols. London, 1891—1899.

949 SHIPPEE, Lester B. *Canadian-American Relations, 1849—1874.* New Haven, Conn., 1939.

950 SHORTRIDGE, W. P. "The Canadian-American Frontier during the Rebellion of 1837—1838." *Can Hist Rev*, VII (1926), 13—26.

951 SOULSBY, Hugh Graham. *The Right of Search and the Slave Trade in Anglo-American Relations, 1814—1862.* See **129**.

952 TANSILL, Charles C. *The Canadian Reciprocity Treaty of 1854.* Baltimore, 1922.

953 TIFFANY, Orrin Edward. "The Relations of the United States to the Canadian Rebellion of 1837—1838." *Pub Buffalo Hist Soc*, VIII (1905), 1—147.

954 VAN ALSTYNE, Richard W. "Anglo-American Relations, 1853—1857; British Statesmen on the Clayton-Bulwer Treaty and American Expansion." *Am Hist Rev*, XLII (1937), 491—500.

955 VAN ALSTYNE, Richard W. "The British Right of Search and the African Slave Trade." *J Mod Hist*, II (1940), 37—47.

956 VAN ALSTYNE, Richard W. "John F. Crampton, Conspirator or Dupe?" *Am Hist Rev*, XLI (1936), 492–502.

957 WASHBURN, Israel. *The Northeastern Boundary*. Portland, Maine, 1881.

958 WATT, Alastair. "The Case of Alexander McLeod." *Can Hist Rev*, XII (1931), 145–167.

959 WEBSTER, C. K. *The Foreign Policy of Palmerston, 1830–1841*. London, 1951.

960 WHITE, Laura A. "The United States in the 1850's As Seen by British Consuls." *Miss Val Hist Rev*, XIX (1933), 509–536.

961 ZORN, R. J. "Criminal Extradition Menaces the Canadian Haven for Fugitive Slaves, 1841–1861." *Can Hist Rev*, XXXVII (1957), 284–294.

3. Continental Europe

962 BLUMENTHAL, Henry. *A Reappraisal of Franco-American Relations, 1830–1871*. Chapel Hill, N.C., 1959.

963 CASPER, Henry W. *American Attitudes toward the Rise of Napoleon III*. Washington, 1947.

964 CURTI, Merle E. "Austria and the United States, 1848–1852: A Study in Diplomatic Relations." *Smith College Studies in History*, XI, No. 3 (1926), 141–206.

965 CURTI, Merle E. "Young America." *Am Hist Rev*, XXXII (1926), 34–55.

966 CURTIS, E. N. "American Opinion of the French Nineteenth-Century Revolutions." *Am Hist Rev*, XXIX (1924), 249–270.

967 DOWTY, Alan. *The Limits of American Isolation: The United States and the Crimean War*. New York, 1971.

968 EGAN, Clifford L. "Pressure Groups, the Department of State, and the Abrogation of the Russian-American Treaty of 1832." *Proc Am Philos Soc*, CXV (1971), 328–334.

969 GAZLEY, J. G. *American Opinion of German Unification, 1848–1871*. New York, 1926.

970 GOLDER, Frank A. "Russian-American Relations during the Crimean War." *Am Hist Rev*, XXXI (1926), 462–476.

971 GORDON, Leland J. *American Relations with Turkey, 1830–1930: An Economic Interpretation*. See 155.

972 HOEKSTRA, Peter. *Thirty-Seven Years of Holland-American Relations, 1803–1840*. Grand Rapids, Mich., 1916.

973 JONES, Horace Perry. "Southern Opinion on the Crimean War." *J Miss Hist*, XXIX (1967), 95–117.

974 KLAY, Andor. *Daring Diplomacy: The Case of the First American Ultimatum*. Minneapolis, Minn., 1957.

975 LERSKI, Jerzy Jan. *A Polish Chapter in Jacksonian America: The United States and the Polish Exiles of 1831.* Madison, Wis., 1958.

976 McGRANE, Reginald C. "The American Position on the Revolution of 1848 in Germany." *Hist Outlook,* XI (1920), 333–339.

977 McLEMORE, Richard Aubrey. *The French Spoilation Claims, 1816– 1836: A Study in Jacksonian Diplomacy.* Nashville, Tenn., 1933.

978 MARRARO, Howard R. *American Opinion on the Unification of Italy, 1846– 1861.* New York, 1932.

979 MARRARO, Howard R. *Diplomatic Relations Between the United States and the Kingdom of the Two Sicilies, 1816– 1861.* New York, 1951.

980 MAY, Arthur James. *Contemporary American Opinion of the Mid-Century Revolutions in Central Europe.* Philadelphia, 1927.

981 MOORE, John Bassett. "Kossuth: A Sketch of Revolutionist." *Pol Sci Q,* X (1895), 257–291.

982 OLIVER, J. W. "Louis Kossuth's Appeal to the Middle West—1852." *Miss Val Hist Rev,* XIV (1928), 481–495.

983 ROONEY, J. William, Jr. "The Diplomatic Mission of Henry Washington Hilliard to Belgium, 1842– 1844." *Ala Hist Q,* XXX (1968), 19–31.

984 SPENCER, Donald S. "Lewis Cass and Symbolic Intervention: 1848– 1852." *Mich Hist,* LIII (1969), 1– 17.

985 SPENCER, Donald S. "Hawks and Doves in the 1850's: Stockton vs. Miller." *NJ Hist,* LXXXVIII (1970), 99– 109.

986 SPENCER, Donald S. "Louis Kossuth and Young America." Doctoral dissertation, University of Virginia, 1973.

987 THOMAS, Benjamin P. *Russo-American Relations, 1815– 1867.* See **149**.

988 WEBSTER, C. K. "British Mediation between France and the United States, 1834– 36." *Eng Hist Rev,* XLII (1927), 58– 78.

4. Latin America and the Caribbean

989 ALLEN, Cyril. "Felix Belly: Nicaraguan Canal Promoter." *His Am Hist Rev,* XXXVII (1957), 46– 59.

990 AMBACHER, Bruce. "George M. Dallas, Cuba, and the Election of 1856." *Pa Mag Hist and Biog,* XCVII (1973), 318–332.

991 BOURNE, Kenneth. "The Clayton-Bulwer Treaty and the Decline of British Opposition to the Territorial Expansion of the United States, 1857– 60." *J Mod Hist,* XXXIII (1961), 287– 291.

992 CALDWELL, R. G. *The López Expeditions to Cuba, 1848– 1851.* Princeton, N.J., 1915.

993 CALLAHAN, James M. *American Foreign Policy in Mexican Relations.* See **196**.

994 CALLCOTT, Wilfred Hardy. *Santa Anna: The Story of an Enigma Who Once Was Mexico.* Norman, Okla., 1936.

995 CARR, Albert H. *The World and William Walker.* New York,, 1963.

996 ETTINGER, Amos A. *The Mission to Spain of Pierre Soulé, 1853– 1855: A Study in the Cuban Diplomacy of the United States.* New Haven, Conn., 1932.

997 FONER, Philip S. *A History of Cuba and Its Relations with the United States.* See **202**.

998 GOOCH, B. D. "Belgium and the Prospective Sale of Cuba in 1837." *His Am Hist Rev,* XXXIX (1959), 413–427.

999 HENDERSON, G. B. "Southern Designs on Cuba, 1854–1857, and Some European Opinions." *J S Hist,* V (1939), 371–385.

1000 HOWE, George F. "The Clayton-Bulwer Treaty: An Unofficial Interpretation of Article VIII in 1869." *Am Hist Rev,* XLII (1937), 484–490.

1001 HUDSON, Randall O. "The Filibuster Minister: The Career of John Hill Wheeler as United States Minister to Nicaragua, 1854–1856." *N Car Hist Rev,* XLIX (1972), 280–297.

1002 JANES, Henry Lorenzo. "The Black Warrior Affair." *Am Hist Rev,* XII (1907), 280–298.

1003 KARNES, Thomas L. *The Failure of Union: Central America, 1824– 1960.* Chapel Hill, N.C., 1961.

1004 KATZ, Irving. "August Belmont's Cuban Acquisition Scheme." *Mid-Am,* L (1968), 52–63.

1005 MANNING, William R. *Early Diplomatic Relations between the United States and Mexico.* Baltimore, 1916.

1006 MAY, Robert E. *The Southern Dream of a Caribbean Empire, 1854– 1861.* Baton Rouge, La., 1973.

1007 PERKINS, Dexter. *The Monroe Doctrine, 1826– 1867.* Baltimore, 1933.

1008 RAUCH, Basil. *American Interest in Cuba: 1848– 1855.* New York, 1948.

1009 RIPPY, J. Fred. *Latin America in World Politics: An Outline Survey.* New York, 1928.

1010 RIVES, George L. *The United States and Mexico, 1821– 1848.* 2 vols. New York, 1913.

1011 RODRIGUEZ, Mario. *A Palmerstonian Diplomat in Central America: Frederic Chatfield, Esq.* Tucson, Ariz., 1964.

1012 RODRIGUEZ, Mario. "The 'Prometheus' and the Clayton-Bulwer Treaty." *J Mod Hist,* XXXVI (1964), 260–278.

1013 SCROGGS, W. O. *Filibusters and Financiers.* New York, 1916.

1014 SHERMAN, William R. *The Diplomatic and Commercial Relations of the United States and Chile, 1820– 1914.* Boston, 1926.

1015 TANSILL, Charles C. *The United States and Santo Domingo, 1798– 1873.* Baltimore, 1938.

1016 URBAN, C. S. "The Abortive Quitman Filibustering Expedition, 1853– 1855." *J Miss Hist,* XVIII (1956), 175–196.

1017 URBAN, C. S. "The Africanization of Cuba Scare, 1853–1855." *His Am Hist Rev,* XXXVII (1957), 29–45.

1018 VAN ALSTYNE, Richard W. "British Diplomacy and the Clayton-Bulwer Treaty, 1850 – 1860." *J Mod Hist*, XI (1939), 149 – 183.

1019 VAN ALSTYNE, Richard W. "The Central American Policy of Lord Palmerston, 1846 – 1848." *His Am Hist Rev*, XVI (1936), 339 – 359.

1020 WILSON, Howard Lafayette. "President Buchanan's Proposed Intervention in Mexico." *Am Hist Rev*, V (1900), 687 – 701.

5. Asia, the Pacific, and the Middle East

1021 BRADLEY, Harold W. *The American Frontier in Hawaii: The Pioneers, 1789 – 1843.* Stanford, Cal., 1942.

1022 BRYSON, Thomas A. "William Brown Hodgson's Mission to Egypt, 1834." *West Georgia College Studies in the Social Sciences*, XI (1972), 10 – 17.

1023 CLYDE, Paul H. "Historical Reflections on American Relations with the Far East." *S Atl Q*, LXI (1962), 389 – 410.

1024 COSENZA, M. E., ed. *The Complete Journal of Townsend Harris.* New York, 1930.

1025 CROW, Carl. *He Opened the Door of Japan.* New York, 1939.

1026 DOWNS, Jacques M. "American Merchants and the China Opium Trade, 1800 – 1840." *Bus Hist Rev*, XLII (1968), 418 – 442.

1027 DULLES, Foster Rhea. *The Old China Trade.* Boston, 1930.

1028 FAIRBANK, John K. *Trade and Diplomacy on the China Coast: The Opening of the Treaty Ports, 1842 – 1854.* Cambridge, Mass., 1953.

1029 FOSTER, John W. *American Diplomacy in the Orient.* Boston, 1930.

1030 FUESS, Claude M. *The Life of Caleb Cushing.* New York, 1923.

1031 GABARD, William M. "John Elliott Ward and the Treaty of Tientsin." *West Georgia College Studies in the Social Sciences*, XI (1972), 26 – 44.

1032 GORDON, Leonard. "Early American Relations with Formosa, 1849 – 1870." *The Historian*, XIX (1957), 262 – 289.

1033 GRIFFIN, Eldon. *Clippers and Consuls: American Consular and Commercial Relations with Eastern Asia, 1845 – 1860.* Ann Arbor, Mich., 1938.

1034 HAWKS, F. L. *Narrative of the Expedition of an American Squadron to the China Seas and Japan.* New York, 1856.

1035 IRICK, Robert L., and K. C. LIU. *American-Chinese Relations, 1784 – 1941: A Survey of Chinese Materials at Harvard.* Cambridge, Mass., 1960.

1036 KUEBEL, Mary V. "Merchants and Mandarins: The Genesis of American Relations with China." Doctoral dissertation, University of Virginia, 1974.

1037 KUO, P. C. "Caleb Cushing and the Treaty of Wanghia, 1844." *J Mod Hist*, V (1933), 34 – 54.

1038 KUYKENDALL, Ralph Simpson. *The Hawaiian Kingdom, 1778—1854.* Honolulu, 1938.

1039 LATOURETTE, Kenneth Scott. *The History of Early Relations between the United States and China, 1784—1844.* New Haven, Conn., 1917.

1040 LUBBOCK, Basil. *The China Clippers.* Glasgow, 1922.

1041 MORGAN, Theodore. *Hawaii: A Century of Economic Change, 1778—1876.* Cambridge, Mass., 1948.

1042 MORISON, Samuel Eliot. *"Old Bruin": Commodore Matthew C. Perry, 1794—1858.* Boston, 1968.

1043 NEUMANN, William L. *America Encounters Japan: From Perry to MacArthur.* Baltimore, 1963.

1044 NEUMANN, William L. "Religion, Morality, and Freedom: The Ideological Background of the Perry Expedition." *Pac Hist Rev,* XXIII (1954), 247—257.

1045 PHILLIPS, Clifton Jackson. *Protestant American and the Pagan World: The First Half Century of the American Board of Commissioners for Foreign Missions, 1810—1860.* Cambridge, Mass., 1969.

1046 PINEAU, Roger, ed. *The Japan Expedition, 1852—1854: The Personal Journal of Commodore Matthew C. Perry.* Washington, 1968.

1047 SHARROW, Walter G. "William Henry Seward and the Basis for American Empire, 1850—1860." *Pac Hist Rev,* XXXVI (1967), 325—342.

1048 STRAUSS, W. P. "Pioneer American Diplomats in Polynesia, 1820—1840." *Pac Hist Rev,* XXXI (1962), 21—30.

1049 SWISHER, Earl, trans. *China's Management of the American Barbarians: A Study of Sino-American Relations, 1841—1861, with Documents.* New Haven, Conn., 1953.

1050 SZCZESNIAK, Boleslaw, ed. *The Opening of Japan: Diary of George Henry Preble, A Diary of Discovery in the Far East, 1853—1856.* Norman, Okla., 1962.

1051 TATE, Merze. "Slavery and Racism as Deterrents to the Annexation of Hawaii, 1854—1855." *J Neg Hist,* XLVII (1962), 1—18.

1052 TONG, Te-kong. *United States Diplomacy in China, 1844—1860.* Seattle, Wash., 1964.

1053 TREAT, Payson J. *Diplomatic Relations between the United States and Japan, 1853—1905.* 3 vols. Stanford, Cal., 1932—1938.

1054 TSIANG, T. F. "The Extension of Equal Commercial Privileges to Other Nations than the British after the Treaty of Nanking." *Chinese Soc and Pol Sci Rev,* XV (1931), 422—444.

1055 VAN DER CORPUT, Jeannette C., and Robert A. WILSON, trans. and eds. *Japan Journal: 1855—1861.* New Brunswick, N.J., 1964. Journal of Henry Heusken.

1056 VERNON, M. C. "The Dutch and the Opening of Japan by the United States." *Pac Hist Rev,* XXVIII (1959), 39—48.

1057 WALWORTH, Arthur. *Black Ships off Japan: The Story of Commodore Perry's Expedition.* New York, 1946.

1058 YANAGA, Chitoshi. *"The First Japanese Embassy to the United States."* *Pac Hist Rev,* IX (1940), 113—138.

VII. Continental Expansion

1. General Studies

1059 BARRAGY, Terrence J. "The Trading Age, 1792–1844." *Oregon Hist Q,* LXXVI (1975), 197–224.

1060 BENTON, Thomas Hart. *Thirty Years' View.* 2 vols. New York, 1854–1856.

1061 BILLINGTON, Ray A. *The Far Western Frontier, 1830–1860.* New York, 1956.

1062 BILLINGTON, Ray A. *Westward Extension: A History of the American Frontier.* New York, 1949.

1063 CLELAND, Robert Glass. "Asiatic Trade and the American Occupation of the Pacific Coast." *Ann Rep Am Hist Assn for the Year 1914,* I (1916), 281–289.

1064 DeVOTO, Bernard. *The Year of Decision: 1846.* Boston, 1943.*

1065 GARRISON, George P. *Westward Extension: 1841–1850.* New York, 1906.

1066 GOETZMANN, William H. *When the Eagle Screamed: The Romantic Horizon in American Diplomacy, 1800–1860.* New York, 1966.*

1067 GRAEBNER, Norman A. *Empire on the Pacific: A Study in American Continental Expansion.* New York, 1955.

1068 GRAEBNER, Norman A., ed. *Manifest Destiny.* Indianapolis, 1968.*

1069 JORDAN, H. Donaldson. "A Politician of Expansion: Robert J. Walker." *Miss Val Hist Rev,* XIX (1933), 362–381.

1070 KUSHNER, Howard I. "Visions of the Northwest Coast: Gwin and Seward in the 1850s." *Western Hist Q,* IV (1973), 295–306.

1071 McELROY, Robert McNutt. *The Winning of the Far West: A History of the Regaining of Texas, of the Mexican War, of the Oregon Question, and of the Successive Additions to the Territory of the United States, within the Continent of America: 1829–1867.* New York, 1914.

1072 MERK, Frederick. *Fruits of Propaganda in the Tyler Administration.* Cambridge, Mass., 1971.

1073 MERK, Frederick. *Manifest Destiny and Mission in American History: A Reinterpretation.* New York, 1963.*

1074 MERK, Frederick. *The Monroe Doctrine and American Expansionism, 1843–1849.* New York, 1966.

1075 MORISON, Samuel Eliot. *Maritime History of Massachusetts, 1783–1860.* Boston, 1923.

1076 PARISH, J. C. *The Emergence of the Idea of Manifest Destiny.* Los Angeles, Cal., 1932.

1077 PLETCHER, David M. *The Diplomacy of Annexation: Texas, Oregon, and the Mexican War.* Columbia, Mo., 1973.

1078 PRATT, Julius W. "The Origin of 'Manifest Destiny.' " *Am Hist Rev*, XXXII (1927), 795—798.

1079 SELLERS, Charles G. *James K. Polk, Continentalist: 1843— 1846.* Princeton, N.J., 1964.

1080 WEINBERG, Albert K. *Manifest Destiny: A Study of Nationalist Expansionism in American History.* See **109.**

1081 WILSON, Major L. "Manifest Destiny and Free Soil: The Triumph of Negative Liberalism in the 1840's." *The Historian*, XXXI (1968), 36—56.

2. Texas

1082 ADAMS, Ephraim Douglas. *British Interests and Activities in Texas, 1838— 1846.* Baltimore, 1910.

1083 BANCROFT, Hubert Howe. *History of the North Mexican States and Texas.* 2 vols. San Francisco, Cal., 1884— 1889.

1084 BARKER, E. C. *Mexico and Texas, 1821— 1835.* Dallas, Tex., 1928.

1085 BARKER, Nancy N. "Devious Diplomat: Dubois de Saligny and the Republic of Texas." *Southwestern Hist Q*, LXXII (1969), 324— 334.

1086 BINKLEY, William C., ed. *Official Correspondence of the Texas Revolution, 1835— 1836.* 2 vols. New York, 1936.

1087 BINKLEY, William C. *The Texas Revolution.* Baton Rouge, La., 1952.

1088 BRAUER, KINLEY J. "The Massachusetts State Texas Committee: A Last Stand against the Annexation of Texas." *J Am Hist*, LI (1964), 220—236.

1089 CASTEÑEDA, Carlos E., trans. and ed. *The Mexican Side of the Texas Revolution. . . .* Dallas, Tex., 1928.

1090 DAY, Donald, and H. H. ULLOM. *The Autobiography of Sam Houston.* Norman, Okla., 1954.

1091 FRIEND, Llerena. *Sam Houston: The Great Designer.* Austin, Tex., 1954.

1092 GAMBRELL, Herbert Pickens. *Anson Jones: The Last President of Texas.* New York, 1948.

1093 GARRISON, George P., ed. *Diplomatic Correspondence of the Republic of Texas. Ann Rep Am Hist Assn for 1907 and 1908.* Washington, 1908, 1911.

1094 GARRISON, George P. *Texas: A Contest of Civilizations.* New York, 1903.

1095 HALL, C. H. "Abel P. Upshur and the Navy as an Instrument of Foreign Policy." *Va Mag of Hist and Biog*, LXIX (1961), 290—299.

1096 JONES, Anson. *Memoranda and Official Correspondence Relating to the Republic of Texas, Its History and Annexation.* New York, 1859.

1097 LAURENT, P. H. "Belgium's Relations with Texas and the United States, 1839—1844." *Southwestern Hist Q*, LXVIII (1964), 220—236.

1098 MANNING, William R. "Texas and the Boundary Issue, 1822—1829." *Southwestern Hist Q*, XVII (1914), 217—261.

1099 MERK, Frederick. *Slavery and the Annexation of Texas.* New York, 1972.

1100 NANCE, Joseph M. *After San Jacinto: The Texas-Mexican Frontier, 1836—1841.* Austin, Tex., 1963.

1101 NANCE, Joseph M. *Attack and Counter-Attack: The Texas-Mexican Frontier, 1842.* Austin, Tex., 1964.

1102 SCHMITZ, Joseph W. *Texan Statecraft, 1836—1845.* San Antonio, Tex., 1941.

1103 SIEGEL, Stanley. *A Political History of the Texas Republic, 1836—1845.* Austin, Tex., 1956.

1104 SMITH, Justin H. *The Annexation of Texas.* New York, 1911.

1105 SMITHER, Harriet. "English Abolitionism and the Annexation of Texas." *Southwestern Hist Q*, XXXII (1929), 193—205.

1106 STENBERG, Richard R. "Jackson, Anthony Butler and Texas." *Southwestern Soc Sci Q*, XIII (1932), 264-286.

1107 STENBERG, Richard R. "President Polk and the Annexation of Texas." *Southwestern Soc Sci Q*, XIV (1934), 336—356.

1108 STENBERG, Richard R. "Intrigue for Annexation." *Southwest Review*, XXV (1939), 58—69.

1109 STEPHENSON, Nathaniel W. *Texas and the Mexican War.* New Haven, Conn., 1921.

1110 VALADES, José C. *Santa Anna y la Guerra de Texas.* Mexico City, 1935.

3. Oregon

1111 BLUE, George Vern. "France and the Oregon Question." *Oregon Hist Q*, XXXIV (1933), 39—59, 144—163.

1112 BLUE, Verne. "The Oregon Question, 1818—1828: A Study of Dr. John Floyd's Efforts in Congress to Secure the Oregon Country." *Oregon Hist Q*, XXIII (1922), 193—219.

1113 CLARK, Robert C., ed. "Aberdeen and Peel on Oregon, 1844." *Oregon Hist Q*, XXXIV (1933), 236—240.

1114 CRAMER, Richard S. "British Magazines and the Oregon Question." *Pac Hist Rev*, XXXII (1963), 369—382.

1115 FRANKLIN, John Hope. "The Southern Expansionists of 1846." *J S Hist*, XXV (1959), 323—338.

1116 GALBRAITH, John S. "France as a Factor in the Oregon Negotiations." *Pac Northwest Q*, XLIV (1953), 69—73.

1117 GRAEBNER, Norman A. "Maritime Factors in the Oregon Compromise." *Pac Hist Rev*, XX (1951), 331—345.

1118 GRAEBNER, Norman A. "Politics and the Oregon Compromise." *Pac Northwest Q*, LII (1961), 7—14.

1119 GRAEBNER, Norman A. "Polk, Politics, and Oregon." *Pub E Tenn Hist Soc*, XXIV (1952), 11–25.

1120 HOWE, Daniel Wait. "The Mississippi Valley in the Movement for Fifty-Four Forty or Fight." *Proc Miss Val Hist Assn for the Year 1911-1912* (1912), 99–116.

1121 HUSBAND, Michael B. "Senator Lewis F. Linn and the Oregon Question." *Mo Hist Rev*, LXVI (1971), 1–19.

1122 JACOBS, Melvin C. *Winning Oregon*. Caldwell, Ida., 1938.

1123 JONES, Wilbur D., and J. Chal VINSON. "British Preparedness and the Oregon Settlement." *Pac Hist Rev*, XXII (1953), 353–364.

1124 McCABE, James O. "Arbitration and the Oregon Question." *Can Hist Rev*, XLI (1960), 308–327.

1125 MARTIN, Thomas P. "Free Trade and the Oregon Question, 1842–1846." *Facts and Factors in Economic History: Articles by Former Students of Edwin Francis Gay*. Cambridge, Mass., 1932.

1126 MERK, Frederick. *Albert Gallatin and the Oregon Problem: A Study in Anglo-American Diplomacy*. Cambridge, Mass., 1950.

1127 MERK, Frederick. "The British Corn Crisis of 1845–1846 and the Oregon Treaty." *Ag Hist*, VIII (1934), 95–123.

1128 MERK, Frederick. "British Government Propaganda and the Oregon Treaty." *Am Hist Rev*, XL (1934), 38–62.

1129 MERK, Frederick. "British Party Politics and the Oregon Treaty." *Am Hist Rev*, XXXVII (1932), 653–675.

1130 MERK, Frederick. "The Genesis of the Oregon Question." *Miss Val Hist Rev*, XXXVI (1950), 583–612.

1131 MERK, Frederick. "The Ghost River Caledonia in the Oregon Negotiation of 1818." *Am Hist Rev*, LV (1950), 530–551.

1132 MERK, Frederick. "The Oregon Pioneers and the Boundary Settlement." *Am Hist Rev*, XXIX (1924), 681–699.

1133 MERK, Frederick. "The Oregon Question in the Webster-Ashburton Negotiations." *Miss Val Hist Rev*, XLIII (1956), 379–404.

1134 MERK, Frederick. *The Oregon Question: Essays in Anglo-American Diplomacy and Politics*. Cambridge, Mass., 1967.

1135 MERK, Frederick. "Presidential Fevers." *Miss Val Hist Rev*, XLVII (1960), 3–33.

1136 MILES, Edwin A. " 'Fifty-four Forty or Fight'—An American Political Legend." *Miss Val Hist Rev*, XLIV (1957), 291–309.

1137 PRATT, Julius W. "James Knox Polk and John Bull." *Can Hist Rev*, XXIV (1943), 341–349.

1138 SAGE, Walter N. "The Oregon Treaty of 1846." *Can Hist Rev*, XXVII (1946), 349–367.

1139 SCHAFER, Joseph. "The British Attitude toward the Oregon Question, 1815–1846." *Am Hist Rev*, XVI (1911), 273–299.

1140 SCHUYLER, Robert L. "Polk and the Oregon Compromise." *Pol Sci Q*, XXVI (1911), 444–461.

1141 SCOTT, Leslie M. "Influence of American Settlement upon the Oregon Boundary Treaty of 1846." *Oregon Hist Q*, XXIX (1928), 1—19.

1142 SELLERS, Charles G. *James K. Polk, Continentalist: 1843—1846.* See **1062**.

1143 VAN ALSTYNE, Richard W. "International Rivalries in Pacific Northwest." *Oregon Hist Q*, XLVI (1945), 185—218.

4. The American Interest in California

1144 ADAMS, Ephraim Douglas. "English Interest in the Annexation of California." *Am Hist Rev*, XIV (1909), 744—763.

1145 CLELAND, Robert Glass. *Early Sentiment for the Annexation of California, 1835—1846.* Austin, Tex., 1915.

1146 ENGELSON, Lester G. "Proposals for the Colonization of California by England in Connection with the Mexican Debt to British Bondholders, 1837—1846." *Cal Hist Soc Q*, XVIII (1939), 136—148.

1147 GRAEBNER, Norman A. "American Interest in California, 1845." *Pac Hist Rev*, XXII (1953), 15—27.

1148 HAWGOOD, John A. "The Pattern of Yankee Infiltration in Mexican Alta California, 1821—1846." *Pac Hist Rev*, XXVII (1958), 27—37.

1149 KNAPP, F. A., Jr. "The Mexican Fear of Manifest Destiny in California." *Essays in Mexican History.* Eds. T. E. Cotner and Carlos E. Casteñeda. Austin, Tex., 1958.

1150 MARTI, W. H. *Messenger of Destiny: The California Adventures, 1846—1847, of Archibald H. Gillespie, U.S. Marine Corps.* San Francisco, Cal., 1960.

1151 NASATIR, Abraham P. *French Activities in California.* Stanford, Cal., 1945.

1152 OGDEN, Adele. "Boston Hide Droghers Along California Shores." *Cal Hist Soc Q*, VIII (1929), 289—305.

1153 OGDEN, Adele. *The California Sea Otter Trade, 1784—1848.* Berkeley, Cal., 1941.

1154 POSNER, Russell. "A British Consular Agent in California: The Reports of James A. Forbes, 1843—1846." *Southern Cal Q*, LIII (1971), 101—112.

1155 ROBINSON, Alfred. *Life in California.* New York, 1846.

1156 TAYS, George. "Frémont Had No Secret Instructions." *Pac Hist Rev*, IX (1940), 157—171.

1157 WYLLYS, Rufus Kay. "French Imperialists in California." *Cal Hist Soc Q*, VIII (1929), 116—129.

5. The Mexican War

1158 BAUER, K. Jack. *The Mexican War, 1846—1848.* New York, 1974.

1159 BILL, Alfred H. *Rehearsal for Conflict: The War with Mexico, 1846–1848.* New York, 1947.

1160 BOCHIN, Hal W. "Caleb B. Smith's Opposition to the Mexican War." *Indiana Mag of Hist,* LXIX (1973), 95–114.

1161 BOURNE, Edward G. "The United States and Mexico, 1847–1848." *Am Hist Rev,* V (1900), 491–502.

1162 BRACK, Gene M. "Mexican Opinion, American Racism, and the War of 1846." *Western Hist Q,* I (1970), 161–174.

1163 BRACK, Gene M. *Mexico Views Manifest Destiny, 1821–1846: An Essay on the Origins of the Mexican War.* Albuquerque, N.M., 1975.

1164 BROOKE, G. M., Jr. "The Vest Pocket War of Commodore Jones." *Pac Hist Rev,* XXXI (1962), 217–233.

1165 CHAMBERLIN, E. K. "Nicholas Trist and Baja California." *Pac Hist Rev,* XXXII (1963), 49–63.

1166 CHANEY, Homer Campbell, Jr. "The Mexican–United States War as Seen by Mexican Intellectuals, 1842–1956." Doctoral dissertation, Stanford University, 1959.

1167 CLENDENEN, Clarence C. *Blood on the Border: The United States Army and the Mexican Irregulars.* New York, 1969.

1168 CONNOR, Seymour V., and Odie B. FAULK. *North America Divided: The Mexican War, 1846–1848.* New York, 1971.

1169 DeVOTO, Bernard. *The Year of Decision: 1846.* See **1064**.

1170 DUFOUR, Charles L. *The Mexican War: A Compact History, 1846–1848.* New York, 1968.

1171 FARNHAM, Thomas J. "Nicholas Trist and James Freaner and the Mission to Mexico (1847–1848)." *Ariz and the West,* XI (1969), 247–260.

1172 FULLER, John D. P. *The Movement for the Acquisition of All Mexico, 1846–1848.* Baltimore, 1938.

1173 GRAEBNER, Norman A. "James K. Polk's Wartime Expansionist Policy." *Pub E Tenn Hist Soc,* XXIII (1951), 32–45.

1174 GRAEBNER, Norman A. "Party Politics and the Trist Mission." *J S Hist,* XIX (1953), 137–156.

1175 HANIGHAN, Frank C. *Santa Anna: The Napoleon of the West.* New York, 1934.

1176 HARSTAD, P. T., and R. W. RESH. "The Causes of the Mexican War: A Note on Changing Interpretations." *Ariz and the West,* VI (1964), 289–302.

1177 HENRY, Robert Selph. *The Story of the Mexican War.* New York, 1950.

1178 HUTCHINSON, C. A. "Valentin Gomez Farias and the Movement for the Return of General Santa Anna to Mexico in 1846." *Essays in Mexican History.* Eds. T. E. Cotner and Carlos E. Casteñeda. Austin, Tex., 1958.

1179 KLEIN, Julius. *The Making of the Treaty of Guadaloupe Hidalgo on February 2, 1848.* Berkeley, Cal., 1905.

1180 KOHL, Clayton Charles. *Claims as a Cause of the Mexican War.* New York, 1914.

1181 LOFGREN, Charles A. "Force and Diplomacy, 1846–1848: The View from Washington." *Mil Affairs,* XXXI (1967), 57–64.

1182 NELSON, Anna Kasten. "Secret Agents and Security Leaks: President Polk and the Mexican War." *Jour Q*, LII (1975), 9 – 14, 98.

1183 NORTHRUP, Jack. "The Trist Mission." *J Mex Am Hist*, III (1973), 13 – 31.

1184 PRICE, Glenn W. *Origins of the War with Mexico: The Polk-Stockton Intrigue*. Austin, Tex., 1967.

1185 RAMIREZ, José Fernando. *Mexico during the War with the United States*. Trans. Elliott B. Scherr. Columbia, Mo., 1950.

1186 RAMSEY, Albert C. *The Other Side: Or Notes for the History of the War between Mexico and the United States*. New York, 1850.

1187 REEVES, Jesse S. "The Treaty of Guadalupe Hidalgo." *Am Hist Rev*, X (1905), 309 – 324.

1188 REYNOLDS, Curtis R. "The Deterioration of Mexican-American Diplomatic Relations, 1833 – 1845." *J of the West*, XI (1972), 213 – 224.

1189 RIPPY, J. Fred. "Border Troubles along the Rio Grande, 1848 – 1860." *Southwestern Hist Q*, XXIII (1919), 91 – 111.

1190 SCHEINA, Robert L. "The Forgotten Fleet: The Mexican Navy on the Eve of War, 1845." *Am Neptune*, XXX (1970), 46 – 55.

1191 SCHROEDER, John H. *Mr. Polk's War: American Opposition and Dissent, 1846 – 1848*. Madison, Wis., 1973.

1192 SEARS, Louis Martin. "Nicholas P. Trist, A Diplomat with Ideals." *Miss Val Hist Rev*, XI (1924), 85 – 98.

1193 SINGLETARY, Otis A. *The Mexican War*. Chicago, 1960.

1194 SMITH, Justin H. *The War with Mexico*. 2 vols. New York, 1919.

1195 STENBERG, Richard R. "The Failure of Polk's Mexican War Intrigue of 1845." *Pac Hist Rev*, IV (1935), 39 – 69.

1196 WEBER, R. B., ed. "The Mexican War: Some Personal Correspondence." *Ind Mag of Hist*, LXV (1969), 133 – 139.

1197 WHITESIDE, Henry O. "Winfield Scott and the Mexican Occupation: Policy and Practice. *Mid-Am*, LII (1970), 102 – 118.

6. *The Gadsden Purchase*

1198 GARBER, P. N. *The Gadsden Treaty*. Philadelphia, 1923.

VIII. Diplomacy of The Civil War

1. Northern Diplomacy

1199 ADAMS, Charles Francis. *Charles Francis Adams*. Boston, 1900.

1200 ADAMS, Charles Francis. *Seward and the Declaration of Paris: A Forgotten Diplomatic Episode, April–August 1861.* Boston, 1912.

1201 Adams, charles Francis. "The Trent Affair." *Am Hist Rev,* XVII (1912), 540–562.

1202 ADAMS, Charles Francis. "The Trent Affair." *Proc Mass Hist Soc,* XLV (1911), 35–148.

1203 ADAMS, Henry. *The Education of Henry Adams: An Autobiography.* Boston, 1918.

1204 BAKER, George E., ed. *The Works of William H. Seward.* 5 vols. New York, 1853–1884.

1205 BALDWIN, S. E. "The 'Continuous Voyage' during the Civil War, and Now." *Am J Int Law,* IX (1915), 793–801.

1206 BANCROFT, Frederic. *The Life of William H. Seward.* 2 vols. New York, 1900.

1207 BAXTER, James P., III. "Papers Relating to Belligerent and Neutral Rights, 1861–1865." *Am Hist Rev,* XXXIV (1928), 77–91.

1208 BIGELOW, John. *Retrospections of an Active Life.* 5 vols. New York, 1909–1913.

1209 BLINN, Howard E. "Seward and the Polish Rebellion of 1863." *Am Hist Rev,* XLV (1940), 828–839.

1210 BOROMÉ, Joseph A. "Henry Adams Silenced by the Cotton Famine." *N Eng Q,* XXXIII (1960), 237–240.

1211 CARROLL, Daniel B. "Abraham Lincoln and the Minister to France, 1860–1863." *Lincoln Herald,* LXX (1968), 142–153.

1212 CASE, Lynn M. "La France et l'affaire du 'Trent.' " *Revue Historique,* CCXXVI (1961), 57–86.

1213 CLAPP, Margaret. *Forgotten First Citizen: John Bigelow.* Boston, 1947.

1214 CLAUSSEN, M. P. "Peace Factors in Anglo-American Relations, 1861–1863." *Miss Val Hist Rev,* XXVI (1940), 511–522.

1215 COHEN, Victor H. "Charles Sumner and the *Trent* Affair." *J S Hist,* XXII (1956), 205–219.

1216 COLEMAN, A. P., and M. M. COLEMAN. *The Polish Insurrection of 1863 in the Light of New York Editorial Opinion.* Williamsport, Pa., 1934.

1217 CONSTABLE, A. "Comment on the Trent Affair." *Westminster Rev,* CLVIII (1902), 640–642.

1218 CROOK, D. P. *Diplomacy During the American Civil War.* New York, 1975.

1219 DANA, R. H. "The Trent Affair: An Aftermath." *Proc Mass Hist Soc,* XLV (1912), 508–522.

1220 DAVIDSON, M. B. "A Royal Welcome for the Russian Fleet." *America and Russia: A Century and a Half of Dramatic Encounters.* Ed. Oliver Jensen. New York, 1962.

1221 DUBERMAN, Martin B. *Charles Francis Adams, 1807–1886.* Boston, 1961.

1222 FERRIS, Norman B. *Desperate Diplomacy: William H. Seward's Foreign Policy, 1861.* Knoxville, Tenn., 1976.

1223 FERRIS, Norman B. *The "Trent" Affair: A Diplomatic Crisis.* Knoxville, Tenn., 1977.

1224 FORD, Worthington C., ed. *A Cycle of Adams Letters, 1861–1865*. 2 vols. Boston, 1920.

1225 GILBERT, Benjamin F. "Welcome to the Czar's Fleet: An Incident of Civil War Days in San Francisco." *Cal Hist Soc Q*, XXVI (1947), 13–19.

1226 GRAEBNER, Norman A. "Northern Diplomacy and European Neutrality." *Why the North Won the Civil War*. Ed. David Donald. Baton Rouge, La., 1960.

1227 HAMER, M.B. "Luring Canadian Soldiers into Union Lines during the War between the States." *Can Hist Rev*, XXVII (1946), 150–162.

1228 HARRIS, Thomas L. *The Trent Affair*. Indianapolis, 1896.

1229 JEFFRIES, W. W. "The Civil War Career of Charles Wilkes." *J S Hist*, XI (1945), 324–348.

1230 KIEGER, John H. "Federal Government Propaganda in Great Britain during the American Civil War." *Hist Outlook*, XIX (1929), 204–209.

1231 LYNCH, Sister Claire. *Diplomatic Mission of John Lothrop Motley to Austria, 1861–1867*. Washington, 1944.

1232 MAYNARD, Douglas H. "The Forbes-Aspinwall Mission." *Miss Val Hist Rev*, XLV (1958), 67–89.

1233 MAYNARD, Douglas H. "Union Efforts to Prevent the Escape of the 'Alabama.' " *Miss Val Hist Rev*, XLI (1954), 41–60.

1234 MONAGHAN, Jay. *Diplomat In Carpet Slippers: Abraham Lincoln Deals with Foreign Affairs*. Indianapolis, 1935.

1235 O'CONNOR, T. H. "Lincoln and the Cotton Trade." *Civ War Hist*, VII (1961), 20–35.

1236 OWSLEY, Frank L. "America and the Freedom of the Seas, 1861–1865." *Essays in Honor of William E. Dodd*. Ed. Avery Craven. Chicago, 1935.

1237 OWSLEY, Harriet C. "Henry Shelton Sanford and Federal Surveillance Abroad, 1861–1865." *Miss Val Hist Rev*, XLVIII (1961), 211–228.

1238 PATTOCK, Florence Bangert. "Cassius M. Clay's Mission to Russia: 1861–1862; 1863–1869." *Filson Club Hist Q*, XLIII (1969), 325–344.

1239 POLE, J. R. *Abraham Lincoln and the Working Classes of Britain*. London, 1959.

1240 POMEROY, Earl S. "The Myth after the Russian Fleet, 1863." *New York Hist*, XXXI (1959), 169–176.

1241 RANDALL, James G., and Richard N. CURRENT. *Lincoln, the President*. 4 vols. New York, 1945–1955.

1242 ROBERTSON, James R. *A Kentuckian at the Court of the Tsars: The Ministry of Cassius Marcellus Clay to Russia, 1861–62 and 1863–69*. Berea, Ky., 1935.

1243 SEWARD, Frederick W. *Reminiscences of a War-Time Statesman and Diplomat, 1830–1915*. New York, 1916.

1244 SEWARD, Frederick W. *Seward at Washington as Senator and Secretary of State*. 2 vols. New York, 1891.

1245 SMILEY, D. L. *The Lion of Whitehall: The Life of Cassius Clay*. Madison, Wis., 1962.

1246 SOWLE, Patrick. "A Reappraisal of Seward's Memorandum of April 1, 1861, to Lincoln." *J S Hist*, XXXIII (1967), 234–239.

1247 VAN DEUSEN, Glyndon G. *William Henry Seward.* New York, 1967.

1248 WALLACE, S. A., and F. E. GILLESPIE, eds. *The Journal of Benjamin Moran, 1857–1865.* 2 vols. Chicago, 1949.

1249 WELLES, Gideon. "The Capture and Release of Mason and Slidell." *Galaxy*, XV (1873), 640–651.

1250 WHITRIDGE, Arnold. "The Alabama, 1862–1864: A Crisis in Anglo-American Relations." *Hist Today*, V (1955), 174–185.

1251 WHITRIDGE, Arnold. "The Trent Affair, 1861." *Hist Today*, IV (1954), 394–402.

1252 WINKS, Robin W. "The Creation of a Myth: 'Canadian' Enlistments in the Northern Armies during the American Civil War." *Can Hist Rev*, XXXIX (1958), 24–40.

1253 WOLDMAN, Albert A. *Lincoln and the Russians.* Cleveland, 1952.

2. Southern Diplomacy

1254 BAYLEN, Joseph O., and William W. WHITE, eds. "A. Dudley Mann's Mission in Europe, 1863–1864: An Unpublished Letter to Jefferson Davis." *Va Mag of Hist and Biog*, LXIX (1961), 324–328.

1255 BLUMENTHAL, Henry. "Confederate Diplomacy: Popular Notions and International Realities." *J S Hist*, XXXII (1966), 151–171.

1256 BONHAM, Milledge Louis, Jr. *The British Consuls in the Confederacy.* New York, 1911.

1257 BULLOCH, James D. *The Secret Service of the Confederate States in Europe.* 2 vols. New York, 1959.

1258 CALLAHAN, James M. *Diplomatic History of the Southern Confederacy.* New York, 1964.

1259 CULLOP, Charles P. *Confederate Propaganda in Europe, 1861–1865.* Coral Gables, Fla., 1969.

1260 DIAMOND, William. "Imports of the Confederate Government from Europe and Mexico." *J S Hist*, VI (1940), 470–503.

1261 Du BELLET, Paul Pecquet. *The Diplomacy of the Confederate Cabinet of Richmond and Its Agents Abroad: Being Memorandum Notes Taken in Paris during the Rebellion of the Southern States from 1861–1865.* Ed. William S. Hoole. Tuscaloosa, Ala., 1963.

1262 GENTRY, Judith Fenner. "A Confederate Success in Europe: The Erlanger Loan." *J S Hist*, XXXVI (1970), 157–188.

1263 GILBERT, Benjamin F. "The Confederate Raider Shenandoah." *J of the West*, IV (1965), 169–182.

1264 JAMESON, J. Franklin. "The London Expenditures of the Confederate Secret Service." *Am Hist Rev*, XXXV (1930), 811–824.

1265 JONES, Wilbur D. *The Confederate Rams at Birkenhead.* Tuscaloosa, Ala., 1961.

1266 LOGAN, F. A. "Activities of the Alabama in Asian Waters." *Pac Hist Rev*, XXXI (1962), 143–150.

1267 MAYNARD, Douglas H. "Plotting the Escape of the Alabama." *J S Hist*, XX (1954), 197–209.

1268 MOORE, J. Preston. "Jefferson Davis and Ambrose Dudley Mann." *J Miss Hist*, XIX (1957), 137–153.

1269 OWSLEY, Frank L. *King Cotton Diplomacy.* Chicago, 1959.

1270 RICHARDSON, James D., ed. and comp. *The Messages and Papers of Jefferson Davis and the Confederacy, Including Diplomatic Correspondence, 1861–1865.* New York, 1966.

1271 SEARS, Louis Martin. "A Confederate Diplomat at the Court of Napoleon III." *Am Hist Rev*, XXVI (1921), 255–281.

1272 SEARS, Louis Martin. *John Slidell.* Durham, N.C., 1925.

1273 STOCK, Leo F. "Catholic participation in the Diplomacy of the Southern Confederacy." *Cath Hist Rev*, XVI (1930), 1–18.

1274 TRESCOT, Edward A. "The Confederacy and the Declaration of Paris." *Am Hist Rev*, XXIII (1918), 826–835.

1275 WILLSON, Beckles. *John Slidell and the Confederates in Paris.* New York, 1932.

3. Foreign Attitudes toward the American Civil War

1276 ADAMOV, E. A., ed. "Documents Relating to Russian Policy during the American Civil War." *J Mod Hist*, II (1930), 603–611.

1277 ADAMOV, E. A. "Russia and the United States at the Time of the Civil War." *J Mod Hist*, II (1930), 583–602.

1278 ADAMS, Ephraim Douglas. *Great Britain and the American Civil War.* 2 vols. New York, 1925.

1279 ALLEN, Harry C. *et al. Heard Round the World: The Impact Abroad of the Civil War.* Ed. Harold Hyman. New York, 1969.

1280 BAILEY, Thomas A. "The Russian Fleet Myth Re-examined." *Miss Val Hist Rev*, XXXVIII (1951), 81–90.

1281 BAXTER, James P., III. "Some British Opinions as to Neutral Rights, 1861–1865." *Am J Int Law*, XXIII (1929), 517–537.

1282 BAXTER, James P., III. "The British Government and Neutral Rights, 1861–1865." *Am Hist Rev*, XXXIV (1928), 9–29.

1283 BELOFF, Max. "Great Britain and the American Civil War." *History*, XXXVII (1952), 40–48.

1284 BERNARD, Mountague. *A Historical Account of the Neutrality of Great Britain During the American Civil War*. London, 1870.

1285 BERNATH, Stuart L. "Squall Across the Atlantic: The Peterhoff Episode." *J S Hist*, XXXIV (1968), 382–401.

1286 BERNATH, Stuart L. *Squall Across the Atlantic: American Civil War Prize Cases and Diplomacy*. Berkeley, Cal., 1970.

1287 BIGELOW, John. *France and the Confederate Navy, 1862–1865*. New York, 1888.

1288 BRADY, E. A. "A Reconsideration of the Lancashire 'Cotton Famine.' " *Ag Hist*, XXXVII (1963), 156–162.

1289 BRAUER, Kinley J. "British Mediation and the American Civil War: A Reconsideration." *J S Hist*, XXXVIII (1972), 49–64.

1290 BRAUER, Kinley J. "Gabriel Garcia y Tassara and the American Civil War: A Spanish Perspective." *Civ War Hist*, XXI (1975), 5–27.

1291 CALLAHAN, James M. *Russo-American Relations during the American Civil War*. Morgantown, W.V., 1908.

1292 CARROLL, Daniel B. *Henri Mercier and the American Civil War*. Princeton, N.J., 1972.

1293 CASE, Lynn M., and Warren F. SPENCER. *The United States and France: Civil War Diplomacy*. Philadelphia, 1970.

1294 COLLYER, C. "Gladstone and the American Civil War." *Proc Leeds Philos Soc*, VI (1951), 583–594.

1295 FERRIS, Norman B. "The Prince Consort, 'The Times,' and the 'Trent' Affair." *Civil War Hist*, VI (1960), 152–156.

1296 FOHLEN, Claude. "La Guerre de Secession et le Commerce Franco-Americain." *Revue d'Histoire Moderne et Contemporaine*, VIII (1961), 259–270.

1297 GAVRONSKY, Serge. *The French Liberal Opposition and the American Civil War*. New York, 1968.

1298 GINZBERG, Eli. "The Economics of British Neutrality during the American Civil War." *Ag Hist*, X (1936), 147–156.

1299 GOLDER, Frank A. "The American Civil War through the Eyes of a Russian Diplomat." *Am Hist Rev*, XXVI (1921), 454–463.

1300 GOLDER, Frank A. "The Russian Fleet and the Civil War." *Am Hist Rev*, XX (1915), 801–812.

1301 GRAEBNER, Norman A. "European Interventionism and the Crisis of 1862." *J Ill State Hist Soc*, LXIX)1976), 35–45.

1302 HAWKINS, R. C. "Coming of the Russian Ships in 1863." *N Am Rev*, CLXXVIII (1904), 539–544.

1303 HERNON, Joseph M., Jr. "The Irish Nationalists and Southern Secession." *Civil War Hist*, XII (1966), 43–53.

1304 JENKINS, Brian. *Britain and the War for the Union*. Montreal, Can., 1974.

1305 JONES, Robert H. "Long Live the King?" *Ag Hist*, XXXVII (1963), 166–169.

1306 JONES, Robert H. "Anglo-American Relations, 1861–1865, Reconsidered." *Mid-Am, XLV (1963), 36–49*.

1307 JONES, Wilbur D. "The British Conservatives and the American Civil War." *Am Hist Rev*, LVIII (1953), 527–543.

1308 JORDAN, Donaldson, and Edwin J. PRATT. *Europe and the American Civil War*. Boston, 1931.

1309 KHASIGIAN, Amos. "Economic Factors and British Neutrality, 1861–1865." *The Historian*, XXV (1963), 441–465.

1310 KUSHNER, Howard I. "The Russian Fleet and the American Civil War: Another View." *The Historian*, XXXIV (1972), 633–649.

1311 KUTOLOWSKI, John. "The Effect of the Polish Insurrection of 1863 on American Civil War Diplomacy." *The Historian*, XXVII (1965), 560–577.

1312 LANDON, Fred. "The American Civil War and Canadian Confederation." *Trans Royal Soc Canada*, XXI (1927), 55–62.

1313 LOGAN, F. A. "India—Britain's Substitute for American Cotton, 1861–1865." *J S Hist*, XXIV (1958), 472–480.

1314 MacDONALD, Helen G. *Canadian Public Opinion on the American Civil War*. New York, 1926.

1315 MacLEAN, Guy. "The *Georgian* Affair: An Incident of the American Civil War." *Can Hist Rev*, XLII (1961), 133–144.

1316 MAYNARD, Douglas. "Civil War 'Care': The Mission of the George Griswold." *N Eng Q*, XXXIV (1961), 291–310.

1317 MERLI, Frank J. *Great Britain and the Confederate Navy, 1861–1865*. Bloomington, Inc., 1970.

1318 MORLEY, John M. *The Life of Richard Cobden*. London, 1908.

1319 NAGENGAST, William E. "The Visit of the Russian Fleet to the United States: Were Americans Deceived?" *Russian Review*, VIII (1949), 46–55.

1320 NEWTON, A. P. "Anglo-American Relations during the Civil War, 1860–1865." *The Cambridge History of British Foreign Policy, 1783–1919*, II. Eds. A. W. Ward and G. P. Gooch. New York, 1922.

1321 NEWTON, Lord Thomas W. L. *Lord Lyons: A Record of British Diplomacy*. London, 1913.

1322 PARK, J. H. "The English Workingmen and the American Civil War." *Pol Sci Q*, XXXIX (1924), 432–437.

1323 PARRY, Albert. "Cassius Clay's Glimpse into the Future: Lincoln's Envoy to St. Petersburg Bade the Two Nations Meet in East Asia." *Russian Review*, II (1943), 52–67.

1324 PIERCE, Edward L., ed. "Letters of Richard Cobden to Charles Sumner, 1862–1865." *Am Hist Rev*, II (1897), 306–319.

1325 POMEROY, Earl S. "French Substitutes for American Cotton, 1861–1865." *J S Hist*, IX (1943), 555–560.

1326 ROBERTSON, James I., Jr., ed. "English Views of the Civil War: A Unique Excursion to Virginia, April 2–8, 1865." *Va Mag of Hist and Biog*, LXXVII (1969), 200–212.

1327 RUSSELL, W. H. *My Diary North and South*. London, 1863.

1328 SCHMIDT, Louis B. "The Influence of Wheat and Cotton on Anglo-American Relations during the Civil War." *Iowa J Hist and Pol*, XVI (1918), 400–439.

1329 SIDEMAN, Belle B., and Lillian FRIEDMAN. *Europe Looks at the Civil War.* New York, 1960.

1330 SILVER, Arthur W., ed. "Henry Adams' 'Diary of a Visit to Manchester.' " *Am Hist Rev,* LI (1945), 74–89.

1331 STERN, Philip Van Doren. *When the Guns Roared: World Aspects of the American Civil War.* Garden City, N.Y., 1965.

1332 TRAUTH, Sister Mary Philip. *Italo-American Diplomatic Relations, 1861–1882.* Washington, 1958.

1333 TREVELYAN, George M. *The Life of John Bright.* New York, 1914.

1334 VILLIERS, Brougham, F. J. SHAW, and W. H. CHESSON. *Anglo-American Relations, 1861–1865.* London, 1919.

1335 WALLING, R. A. J., ed. "Bright-Sumner Letters, 1861–1871." *Proc Mass Hist Soc,* XLVI (1912), 93–164.

1336 WALLING, R. A. J., ed. *The Diaries of John Bright.* London, 1930.

1337 WALPOLE, Spencer. *Life of Lord John Russell.* London, 1891.

1338 WEST, W. Reed. *Contemporary French Opinion of the American Civil War.* Baltimore, 1924.

1339 WINKS, Robin W. *Canada and the United States: The Civil War Years.* Baltimore, 1960.

1340 ZORN, R. J. "John Bright and the British Attitude to the American Civil War." *Mid-A,* XXXVIII (1956), 131–145.

4. Mexico and the Monroe Doctrine

1341 ACEVEDO, Javier Pérez de. *Europa y Mexico, 1861–1862.* Havana, 1935.

1342 ANDERSON, William Marshall. *An American in Maximilian's Mexico, 1865–1866.* Ed. Ramon Ruiz. San Marino, Cal., 1959.

1343 AUER, J. Jeffery. "Lincoln's Minister to Mexico." *Ohio State Arch and Hist Q,* LIX (1950), 115–128.

1344 BANCROFT, Frederic. "The French in Mexico and the Monroe Doctrine." *Pol Sci Q,* XI (1896), 30–43.

1345 BERBUSSE, E. J. "The Origins of the McLane-Ocampo Treaty of 1859." *The Americas,* XIV (1958), 223–245.

1346 BOCK, Carl H. *Prelude to Tragedy: The Negotiation and Breakdown of the Tripartite Convention of London, October 31, 1861.* Philadelphia, 1966.

1347 CALLAHAN, James M. *Evolution of Seward's Mexican Policy.* Morgantown, W.V., 1909.

1348 CASE, Lynn M., ed. *French Opinion on the United States and Mexico, 1860–1867.* New York, 1936.

1349 CORTI, Count Egon C. *Maximilian and Charlotte of Mexico.* New York, 1938.

1350 DUNIWAY, Clyde Augustus. "Reasons for the Withdrawal of the French from Mexico." *Ann Rep Am Hist Assn for the Year 1902* (1903), 313 – 328.

1351 FERRIS, Nathan L. "The Relations of the United States with South America during the American Civil War." *His Am Hist Rev*, XXI (1941), 51 – 78.

1352 FOSTER, John W. "Maximilian and His Mexican Empire." *Columbia Historical Society Review*, XIV (1911), 184 – 202.

1353 FRAZER, Robert W. "Maximilian's Propaganda Activities in the United States, 1865 – 1866." *His Am Hist Rev*, XXIV (1944), 4 – 29.

1354 FRAZER, Robert W. "Latin American Projects to Aid Mexico during the French Intervention." *His Am Hist Rev*, XXVIII (1948), 377 – 388.

1355 FRAZER, Robert W. "Trade between California and the Belligerent Powers during the French Intervention in Mexico." *Pac Hist Rev*, XV (1946), 390 – 399.

1356 GOLDWERT, Marvin. "Matías Romero and Congressional Opposition to Seward's Policy toward the French Intervention in Mexico." *The Americas*, XXII (1965), 22 – 40.

1357 HANNA, Kathryn A. "The Roles of the South in the French Intervention in Mexico." *J S Hist*, XX (1954), 3 – 21.

1358 HOBSON, J. A. "Matías Romero and the Monroe Doctrine in the French Invasion of Mexico: 1862 – 1867." Doctoral dissertation, University of Chicago, 1961.

1359 HOSKINS, H. L. "French View of the Monroe Doctrine and the Mexican Expedition." *His Am Hist Rev*, IV (1921), 677 – 689.

1360 LALLY, F. E. *French Opposition to the Mexican Policy of the Second Empire*. Baltimore, 1931.

1361 McCORNACK, Richard B. "James Watson Webb and French Withdrawal from Mexico." *His Am Hist Rev*, XXXI (1951), 274 – 286.

1362 MALLOY, G. W. "The United States and the French Intervention in Mexico, 1861 – 1867." Doctoral dissertation, University of California, 1937.

1363 MILLER, Robert Ryal. "The American Legion of Honor in Mexico." *Pac Hist Rev*, XXX (1961), 229 – 241.

1364 MILLER, Robert Ryal. "Matías Romero: Mexican Minister to the United States during the Juarez-Maximilian Era." *His Am Hist Rev*, XLV (1965), 228 – 245.

1365 PERKINS, Dexter. *The Monroe Doctrine, 1826 – 1867*. See **1007**.

1366 ROBERTSON, William Spence. "The Tripartite Treaty of London." *His Am Hist Rev*, XX (1940), 167 – 189.

1367 ROEDER, Ralph. *Juarez and His Mexico: A Biographical History*. New York, 1947.

1368 SCHOONOVER, Thomas. "John A. Kasson's Opposition to the Lincoln Administration's Mexican Policy." *Annals of Iowa*, XL (1971), 585 – 592.

IX. Hemispheric Relations: 1865–1900

1. General Studies of Postwar American Foreign Relations

1369 ARMSTRONG, William M. *E. L. Godkin and American Foreign Policy, 1865–1900.* New York, 1957.

1370 BARROWS, Chester L. *William M. Evarts: Lawyer, Diplomat, Statesman.* Chapel Hill, N.C., 1941.

1371 BEISNER, Robert L. *From the Old Diplomacy to the New, 1865–1900.* New York, 1975.

1372 BLAINE, James G. *Political Discussions, Legislative, Diplomatic, and Popular, 1856–1886.* Norwich, Conn., 1887.

1373 BURNETTE, Ollen Lawrence, Jr. "The Senate Foreign Relations Committee and the Diplomacy of Garfield, Arthur, and Cleveland." Doctoral dissertation, University of Virginia, 1952.

1374 CAMPBELL, Charles S. *The Transformation of American Foreign Relations, 1865–1900.* New York, 1976.

1375 CURTI, Merle E. "America at the World Fairs, 1851–1893." *Am Hist Rev,* LV (1950), 833–856.

1376 DONALD, David H. *Charles Sumner and the Rights of Man.* New York, 1970.

1377 DULEBOHN, G. R. *Principles of Foreign Policy under the Cleveland Administrations.* Philadelphia, 1941.

1378 DULLES, Foster Rhea. *Prelude to World Power: American Diplomatic History, 1860–1900.* New York, 1965.

1379 DUNCAN, Bingham. *Whitelaw Reid: Journalist, Politician, Diplomat.* Athens, Ga., 1975.

1380 DYER, Brainerd. *The Public Career of William M. Evarts.* Berkeley, Cal., 1933.

1381 EGGERT, Gerald G. *Richard Olney: Evolution of a Statesman.* University Park, Pa., 1974.

1382 FOSTER, John W. *Diplomatic Memoirs.* 2 vols. Boston, 1909.

1383 GRENVILLE, John A. S., and George Berkeley YOUNG. *Politics, Strategy and American Diplomacy: Studies in Foreign Policy, 1873–1917.* See **275**.

1384 GRESHAM, Matilda. *Life of Walter Quintin Gresham, 1832–1895.* 2 vols. Chicago, 1919.

1385 HAMILTON, Gail. *Biography of James G. Blaine.* Norwich, Conn., 1895.

1386 HOAR, George Frisbie. *Autobiography of Seventy Years.* 2 vols. New York, 1903.

1387 HOLBO, Paul S. "Economics, Emotion, and Expansion: An Emerging Foreign Policy." *The Gilded Age*. Ed. H. Wayne Morgan. Rev. ed. Syracuse, N.Y., 1970.*

1388 JAMES, Henry. *Richard Olney and His Public Service*. Boston, 1923.

1389 LaFEBER, Walter. *The New Empire: An Interpretation of American Expansion, 1860—1898*. Ithaca, N.Y., 1963.*

1390 McELROY, Robert McNutt. *Grover Cleveland, The Man and the Statesman: An Authorized Biography*. 2 vols. London, 1923.

1391 McKEE, Delber Lee. "The American Federation of Labor and American Foreign Policy, 1886—1912." Doctoral dissertation, Stanford University, 1952.

1392 MEGARGEE, Richard. "The Diplomacy of John Bassett Moore: Realism in American Foreign Policy." Doctoral dissertation, Northwestern University, 1963.

1393 MUZZEY, David S. *James G. Blaine: A Political Idol of Other Days*. New York, 1934.

1394 NEVINS, Allan. *Grover Cleveland: A Study in Courage*. New York, 1932.

1395 NEVINS, Allan. *Hamilton Fish: The Inner History of the Grant Administration*. New York, 1936.

1396 NEVINS, Allan. *Henry White: Thirty Years of American Diplomacy*. New York, 1930.

1397 PERKINS, Dexter. *The Monroe Doctrine, 1867—1907*. Baltimore, 1937.*

1398 PERKINS, Dexter. *The United States and Latin America*. Baton Rouge, La., 1961.

1399 PHILLIPS, Frances Marie. "John Watson Foster, 1836—1917." Doctoral dissertation, University of New Mexico, 1956.

1400 PLESUR, Milton. *America's Outward Thrust: Approaches to Foreign Affairs, 1865—1890*. DeKalb, Ill., 1971.

1401 PLETCHER, David M. *The Awkward Years: American Foreign Relations under Garfield and Arthur*. Columbia, Mo., 1962.

1402 RANDOLPH, Bessie Carter. "Foreign Bondholders and the Repudiated Debts of the Southern States." *Am J Int Law*, XXV (1931), 63—82.

1403 SCHONBERGER, Howard B. *Transportation to the Seaboard: The "Communication Revolution" and American Foreign Policy, 1860—1900*. Westport, Conn., 1971.

1404 SPETTER, Allan. "Harrison and Blaine: Foreign Policy, 1889—1893." *Ind Mag of Hist*, LXV (1969), 215—227.

1405 TANSILL, Charles C. *The Foreign Policy of Thomas F. Bayard, 1885—1897*. New York, 1940.

1406 TYLER, Alice Felt. *The Foreign Policy of James G. Blaine*. Minneapolis, Minn., 1927.

1407 VOLWILER, Albert T. *The Correspondence between Benjamin Harrison and James G. Blaine, 1882—1893*. Philadelphia, 1940.

1408 VOLWILER, Albert T. "Harrison, Blaine, and Foreign Policy, 1889—1893." *Proc Am Philos Soc*, LXXIX (1938), 637—648.

1409 WHITE, Andrew Dickson. *Autobiography of Andrew Dickson White*. 2 vols. New York, 1905. Includes the 1899 Hague Conference and other diplomatic assignments.

1410 YOUNGER, Edward. *John A. Kasson: Politics and Diplomacy from Lincoln to McKinley*. Iowa City, Iowa, 1955.

2. Canada

1411 BREBNER, John Bartlet. *North Atlantic Triangle: The Interplay of Canada, the United States and Great Britain*. See **114**.

1412 BROWN, Robert Craig. *Canada's National Policy, 1883— 1900: A Study in Canadian-American Relations*. Princeton, N.J., 1964.

1413 CAMPBELL, Charles S., Jr. "American Tariff Interests and the Northeastern Fisheries, 1883—1888." *Can Hist Rev*, XLV (1964), 212—218.

1414 CLARK, Robert C. "The Diplomatic Mission of Sir John Rose, 1871." *Pac Northwest Q*, XXVII (1936), 227—242.

1415 COLQUHOUN, A. H. U. "The Reciprocity Negotiations with the United States in 1869." *Can Hist Rev*, VIII (1927), 233—242.

1416 CREIGHTON, Donald G. "The United States and Canadian Confederation." *Can Hist Rev*, XXXIX (1958), 209—222.

1417 D'ARCY, William. *The Fenian Movement in the United States: 1858— 1886*. Washington, 1947.

1418 DAVIS, H. A. "The Fenian Raid on New Brunswick." *Can Hist Rev*, XXXVI (1955), 316—334.

1419 DeROSIER, Arthur H., Jr. "Importance in Failure: The Fenian Raids of 1866—1871." *Southern Q*, III (1965), 181—197.

1420 DeROSIER, Arthur H., Jr. "The Settlement of the San Juan Controversy." *Southern Q*, IV (1965), 74—88.

1421 FARIS, John T. *The Romance of the Boundaries*. New York, 1926.

1422 GLUEK, Alvin C., Jr. "The Riel Rebellion and Canadian-American Relations." *Can Hist Rev*, XXXVI (1955), 199—221.

1423 HOWAY, F. W., W. N. SAGE, and H. F. ANGUS. *British Columbia and the United States*. Toronto, Can., 1942.

1424 JENKINS, Brian. *Fenians and Anglo-American Relations during Reconstruction*. Ithaca, N.Y., 1969.

1425 LINDSEY, Charles. *Life and Times of William Lyon Mackenzie*. Toronto, Can., 1862.

1426 LOWER, A. R. M. *Colony to Nation: A History of Canada*. Toronto, Can., 1947.

1427 McCABE, James O. *The San Juan Water Boundary Question*. Toronto, Can., 1965.

1428 MILLER, David Hunter. *Northwest Water Boundary: Report of the Experts Summoned by the German Emperor.* Seattle, Wash., 1942.

1429 MILLER, David Hunter. *San Juan Archipelago: Study of the Joint Occupation of San Juan Island.* See **944**.

1430 ROBINSON, Chalfont. *A History of Two Reciprocity Treaties.* New Haven, Conn., 1904.

1431 SENIOR, Hereward. "Quebec and the Fenians." *Can Hist Rev*, XLVIII (1967), 26–44.

1432 SHIPPEE, Lester B. *Canadian-American Relations, 1849–1874.* See **949**.

1433 SMITH, Joe P. *The Republican Expansionists of the Early Reconstruction Era.* Chicago, 1933.

1434 TANSILL, Charles C. *Canadian-American Relations, 1875–1911.* New York, 1943.

1435 TUNEM, Alfred. "The Dispute over the San Juan Island Water Boundary." *Washington Hist Q*, XXIII (1932), 38–46, 133–137, 196–204, 286–300.

1436 WARNER, D. F. "Drang Nach Norden: The United States and the Riel Rebellion." *Miss Val Hist Rev*, XXXIX (1953), 693–712.

1437 WARNER, D. F. *The Idea of Continental Union: Agitation for the Annexation of Canada to the United States, 1849–1893.* See **107**.

3. Mexico, Central America and the Caribbean

1438 CALLAHAN, James M. *Cuba and International Relations: A Historical Study of American Diplomacy.* Baltimore, 1899.

1439 CALLCOTT, Wilfred Hardy. *The Caribbean Policy of the United States, 1890–1920.* Baltimore, 1942.

1440 CHADWICK, French Ensor. *The Relations of the United States and Spain: Diplomacy.* New York, 1909.

1441 CHAPMAN, Mary P. "The Mission of Lansing Bond Mizner to Central America." *The Historian*, XIX (1957), 385–401.

1442 COLE, Cornelius. *Memoirs of Cornelius Cole, Ex-Senator of the United States from California.* New York, 1908. Cole sponsored the annexation of Santo Domingo.

1443 CROWELL, Jackson. "The United States and a Central American Canal, 1869–1877." *His Am Hist Rev*, XLIX (1969), 27–52.

1444 DOUGLASS, Frederick. "Haiti and the United States: Inside History of the Negotiations for the Mole St. Nicolas." *N Am Rev*, CLIII (1891), 337–345.

1445 DuVAL, Miles P., Jr. *Cadiz to Cathay: The Story of the Long Struggle for a Waterway across the American Isthmus.* Stanford, Cal., 1940.

1446 FONER, Philip S. *A History of Cuba and Its Relations with the United States.* See **997**.

1447 GRANT, Ulysses S. "The Nicaragua Canal." *N Am Rev*, CXXXII (1881), 107–116.

1448 GREGG, Robert D. *The Influence of Border Troubles on Relations between the United States and Mexico, 1876–1910.* Baltimore, 1937.

1449 GRENVILLE, John A. S. "Great Britain and the Isthmian Canal, 1898–1901." *Am Hist Rev*, LXI (1955), 48–69.

1450 HACKETT, Charles W. "The Recognition of the Diaz Government by the United States." *Southwestern Hist Q*, XXVIII (1924), 34–55.

1451 HARDY, Osgood. "Ulysses S. Grant, President of the Mexican Southern Railroad." *Pac Hist Rev*, XXIV (1955), 111–120.

1452 HEPBURN, William P. "The Nicaragua Canal." *Independent*, LII (1900), 294–296.

1453 HIMELHOCH, Myra. "Frederick Douglass and Haiti's Mole St. Nicolas." *J Neg Hist*, LVI (1971), 161–180.

1454 KEASBEY, Lindley M. *The Nicaragua Canal and the Monroe Doctrine.* New York, 1896.

1455 KOHT, Halvdan. "The Origin of Seward's Plan to Purchase the Danish West Indies." *Am Hist Rev*, L (1945), 762–767.

1456 MACK, Gerstle. *The Land Divided: A History of the Panama Canal and Other Isthmian Canal Projects.* New York, 1944.

1457 PLETCHER, David M. *Rails, Mines, and Progress: Seven American Promoters in Mexico, 1867–1911.* Ithaca, N.Y., 1958.

1458 PLETCHER, David M. "Mexico Opens the Door to American Capital, 1877–1880." *The Americas*, XVI (1959), 1–14.

1459 REED, Thomas B. "The Nicaragua Canal." *N Am Rev*, CLXVIII (1899), 552–562.

1460 RIPPY, J. Fred. "Relations of the United States and Guatemala during the Epoch of Justo Rufino Barrios." *His Am Hist Rev*, XXII (1942), 595–605.

1461 ROMERO, Matías. *Mexico and the United States.* New York, 1898.

1462 ROMERO, Matías. "Mr. Blaine and the Boundary Question between Mexico and Guatemala." *J Am Geog Soc of New York*, XXIX (1897), 281–330.

1463 SEARS, Louis Martin. "Frederick Douglass and the Mission to Haiti, 1889–1891." *His Am Hist Rev*, XXI (1941), 222–238.

1464 SENSABAUGH, Leon F. *American Interest in the Mexican-Guatemalan Boundary Dispute. Birmingham-Southern College Bulletin*, XXXIII. Birmingham, Ala., 1940.

1465 TANSILL, Charles C. *The Purchase of the Danish West Indies.* Baltimore, 1932.

1466 TERRILL, Tom E. *The Tariff, Politics, and American Foreign Policy, 1874–1901.* Westport, Conn., 1973.

1467 VILLEGAS, Daniel Cosio. *The United States versus Porfirio Diaz.* Trans. Nettie Lee Benson. Lincoln, Nebr., 1963.

1468 WILLIAMS, Mary W. *Anglo-American Isthmian Diplomacy, 1815–1915.* See **854**.

4. South America and Pan Americanism

1469 BASTERT, Russell H. "Diplomatic Reversal: Frelinghuysen's Opposition to Blaine's Pan-American Policy in 1882." *Miss Val Hist Rev*, XLII (1956), 653—671.

1470 BASTERT, Russell H. "A New Approach to the Origins of Blaine's Pan-American Policy." *His Am Hist Rev*, XXXIX (1959), 375-412.

1471 BELMONT, Perry *An American Democrat: The Recollections of Perry Belmont.* New York, 1941. On Blaine's policy toward Chile and Peru.

1472 CORTADA, James W. "Diplomatic Rivalry between Spain and the United States over Chile and Peru, 1864-1871." *Inter-Am Econ Affairs*, XXVII (1974), 47-58.

1473 DENNIS, William J. *Tacna and Arica: An Account of the Chile-Peru Boundary Dispute and of the Arbitrations by the United States.* New Haven, Conn., 1931.

1474 EISTER, Allan W. *The United States and the A. B. C. Powers, 1889—1906.* Dallas, 1950.

1475 EVANS, H. C., Jr. *Chile and Its Relations with the United States.* Durham, N.C., 1927.

1476 HARDY, Osgood. "Was Patrick Egan a 'Blundering Minister'?" *His Am Hist Rev*, VIII (1928), 65—81.

1477 HARDY, Osgood. "The Itata Incident." *His Am Hist Rev*, V (1922), 195—226.

1478 HILL, Lawrence F. *Diplomatic Relations between the United States and Brazil.* See **205**.

1479 LaFEBER, Walter. "United States Depression Diplomacy and the Brazilian Revolution, 1893—1894." *His Am Hist Rev*, XL (1960), 107—118.

1480 LINDSELL, Harold. *The Chilean-American Controversy of 1891—1892.* New York, 1943.

1481 LOCKEY, J. B. *Pan-Americanism: Its Beginnings.* New York, 1920.

1482 McGANN, Thomas F. *Argentina, the United States, and the Inter-American System, 1880—1914.* Cambridge, Mass., 1957.

1483 MECHAM, J. Lloyd. *The United States and Inter-American Security, 1889—1960.* Austin, Tex., 1961.

1484 MILLINGTON, Herbert. *American Diplomacy and the War of the Pacific.* New York, 1948.

1485 RIPPY, J. Fred. *Latin America in World Politics: An Outline Survey.* See **1009**.

1486 ROMERO, Matías. "The Pan-American Conference." *N Am Rev*, CLI (1890), 354—366.

1487 SHERMAN, William R. *The Diplomatic and Commercial Relations of the United States and Chile, 1820—1914.* See **1014**.

1488 TIMM, Charles A. "The Diplomatic Relations between the United States and Brazil during the Naval Revolt of 1893." *Southwest Pol and Soc Sci Q*, V (1924), 119—138.

1489 VIVIAN, James F. "The Commercial Bureau of the American Republics, 1894—1902: The Advertising Policy, the State Department, and the Governance of the International Union." *Proc Am Philos Soc*, CXVIII (1974), 555—566.

1490 WILGUS, A. C. "James G. Blaine and the Pan-American Movement." *His Am Hist Rev*, V (1922), 662—708.

5. The Venezuela Boundary Controversy

1491 BAKER, Marcus. "The Venezuelan Boundary Commission and Its Work." *Nat Geog Mag*, VIII (1897), 193—201.

1492 BLAKE, Nelson M. "Background of Cleveland's Venezuelan Policy." *Am Hist Rev*, XLVII (1942), 259—277.

1493 BLAKE, Nelson M. "The Olney-Pauncefote Treaty of 1897." *Am Hist Rev*, L (1945), 228—243.

1494 BRYCE, James. "British Feeling on the Venezuelan Question." *N Am Rev*, CLXII (1896), 145—153.

1495 CARNEGIE, Andrew. "The Venezuelan Question." *N Am Rev*, CLXII (1896), 129—144.

1496 CHILD, Clifton J. "The Venezuela-British Guiana Boundary Arbitration of 1899." *Am J Int Law*, XLIV (1950), 682—693.

1497 CLEVELAND, Grover. *Presidential Problems*. New York, 1904. Includes a long chapter on Venezuela.

1498 CLEVELAND, Grover. *The Venezuelan Boundary Controversy*. Princeton, N.J., 1913.

1499 COUDERT, Frederic R. "The Anglo-American Arbitration Treaty." *Forum*, XXIII (1897), 13—22.

1500 DENNIS, William Cullen. "The Venezuela-British Guiana Boundary Arbitration of 1899." *Am J Int Law*, XLIV (1950), 720—727.

1501 FENTON, P. F. "Diplomatic Relations of the United States and Venezuela, 1880-1915." *His Am Hist Rev*, VIII (1928), 330-356.

1502 FOSSUM, Paul R. "The Anglo-Venezuelan Boundary Controversy." *His Am Hist Rev*, VIII (1928), 299-329.

1503 GRENVILLE, John A. S. *Lord Salisbury and Foreign Policy: The Close of the Nineteenth Century*. London, 1964.

1504 JERVEY, Theodore D. "William Lindsay Scruggs—A Forgotten Diplomat." *S Atl Q*, XXVII (1928), 292-309.

1505 LaFEBER, Walter. "The American Business Community and Cleveland's Venezuelan Message." *Bus Hist Rev*, XXXIV (1960), 393-402.

1506 LaFEBER, Walter. "The Background of Cleveland's Venezuelan Policy: A Reinterpretation." *Am Hist Rev*, LXVI (1961), 947—967.

1507 LaFEBER, Walter. "The Latin American Policy of the Second Cleveland Administration." Doctoral dissertation, University of Wisconsin, 1959.

1508 LODGE, Henry Cabot. "England, Venezuela, and the Monroe Doctrine." *N Am Rev*, CLX (1895), 651—658.

1509 MATHEWS, Joseph J. "Informal Diplomacy in the Venezuela Crisis of 1896." *Miss Val Hist Rev*, L (1963), 195—212.

1510 PHELPS, Edward J. "Arbitration and Our Relations with England." *Atl Mon*, LXXVIII (1896), 26—34.

1511 RIPPY, J. Fred. "Some Contemporary Mexican Reactions to Cleveland's Venezuelan Message." *Pol Sci Q*, XXXIX (1924), 280—292.

1512 SCHOENRICH, Otto. "The Venezuela-British Guiana Boundary Dispute." *Am J Int Law*, XLIII (1949), 523—530.

1513 SCRUGGS, William L. *British Aggressions in Venezuela; or, The Monroe Doctrine on Trial*. Atlanta, Ga., 1895.

1514 SCRUGGS, William L. "The Monroe Doctrine—Its Origins and Import." *N Am Rev*, CLXXVI (1903), 185—199.

1515 SLOAN, Jennie A. "Anglo-American Relations and the Venezuelan Boundary Dispute." *His Am Hist Rev*, XVIII (1938), 486—506.

1516 SMITH, Theodore C. "Secretary Olney's Real Credit in the Venezuelan Affair." *Proc Mass Hist Soc*, LXV (1933), 112—147.

1517 STRAUS, Oscar S. "Lord Salisbury and the Monroe Doctrine." *Forum*, XX (1896), 713—720.

1518 WOOLSEY, Theodore S. "The President's Monroe Doctrine." *Forum*, XX (1896), 705—712.

1519 YOUNG, George Berkeley. "Intervention Under the Monroe Doctrine: The Olney Corollary." *Pol Sci Q*, LVII (1942), 247—280.

X. Europe, the Mediterranean, and Africa: 1865–1900

1. Great Britain

1520 ADAMS, George B. "The United States and the Anglo-Saxon Future." *Atl Mon*, LXXVIII (1896), 35—44.

1521 BAXTER, James P., III. "The British High Commissioners at Washington in 1871." *Proc Mass Hist Soc*, LXV (1934), 334—357.

1522 BESANT, Walter. "The Future of the Anglo-Saxon Race." *N Am Rev*, CLXIII (1896), 129—143.

1523 BLAKE, Nelson M. "England and the United States, 1897—1899." *Essays in History and International Relations in Honor of George Hubbard Blakeslee*. Eds. D. E. Lee and G. E. McReynolds. Worcester, Mass., 1949.

1524 BOURNE, Kenneth. *Britain and the Balance of Power in North America, 1815—1908.* See **914**.

1525 BOUTWELL, George S. *Reminiscences of Sixty Years in Public Affairs.* 2 vols. New York, 1902. The Treaty of Washington and the Senate.

1526 BROWN, Thomas N. *Irish-American Nationalism, 1870—1890.* Philadelphia, 1966.

1527 BRYCE, James. "The Essential Unity of Britain and America." *Atl Mon,* LXXXII (1898), 22—29.

1528 BURTON, David Henry. "Theodore Roosevelt and His English Correspondents: The Intellectual Roots of the Anglo-American Alliance." *Mid-Am,* LIII (1971), 12—34.

1529 BURTON, David Henry. *Theodore Roosevelt and His English Correspondents: A Special Relationship of Friends.* Philadelphia, 1973.

1530 CAMPBELL, Alexander E. *Great Britain and the United States, 1895—1903.* London, 1960.

1531 CAMPBELL, Charles S., Jr. *Anglo-American Understanding, 1898—1903.* Baltimore, 1957.

1532 CAMPBELL, Charles S., Jr. "The Anglo-American Crisis in the Bering Sea, 1890—1891." *Miss Val Hist Rev,* XLVIII (1961), 393—414.

1533 CAMPBELL, Charles S., Jr. "Anglo-American Relations, 1897—1901." *Threshold to American Internationalism.* See **1861**.

1534 CAMPBELL, Charles S., Jr. "The Bering Sea Settlements of 1892." *Pac Hist Rev,* XXXII (1963), 347—367.

1535 CAMPBELL, Charles S., Jr. "The Dismissal of Lord Sackville." *Miss Val Hist Rev,* XLIV (1958), 635—648.

1536 CAMPBELL, Charles S., Jr. "American Tariff Interests and the Northeastern Fisheries, 1883—1888." *Can Hist Rev,* XLV (1964), 212—228.

1537 CAMPBELL, Charles S., Jr. "Edward J. Phelps and Anglo-American Relations." *Contrast and Connections: Bicentennial Essays in Anglo-American History.* Eds. Harry C. Allen and Roger F. Thompson. London, 1976.

1538 CARNEGIE, Andrew. "Does America Hate England?" *Contemporary Rev,* LXXIII (1897), 660—668.

1539 CHAMBERLAIN, Joseph. "Recent Developments of Policy in the United States and Their Relation to an Anglo-American Alliance." *Scribner's Mag,* XXIV (1898), 674—682.

1540 COOK, Adrian. *The Alabama Claims, American Politics and Anglo-American Relations, 1865—1872.* Ithaca, N.Y., 1975.

1541 CRAPOL, Edward P. *America for Americans: Economic Nationalism and Anglophobia in the Late Nineteenth Century.* Westport, Conn., 1973.

1542 CUSHING, Caleb. *The Treaty of Washington: Its Negotiation, Execution, and the Discussions Relating Thereto.* New York, 1873.

1543 DAVIS, John C. Bancroft. *Mr. Fish and the Alabama Claims: A Chapter in Diplomatic History.* Boston, 1893.

1544 DICEY, A. V. "England and America." *Atl Mon,* LXXXII (1898), 441—445.

1545 DILKE, Charles W. "The Future Relations of Great Britain and the United States." *Forum,* XXVI (1899), 521—528.

1546 DOS PASSOS, John R. *The Anglo-Saxon Century and the Unification of the English-Speaking People.* New York, 1903.

1547 EDMUNDS, George F. "The Fishery Award." *N Am Rev*, CXXVIII (1879), 1−14.

1548 EDWARDS, Owen D. "American Diplomats and Irish Coercion, 1880−1883." *J Am Stud*, I (1967), 213−232.

1549 FERGUSON, John H. *American Diplomacy and the Boer War.* Philadelphia, 1939.

1550 FISH, Carl Russell. *The United States and Great Britain.* Chicago, 1932.

1551 FITZMAURICE, Lord Edmond. *The Life of Granville, George Leveson Gower, Second Earl Granville, K.G., 1815−1891.* 2 vols. London, 1905. Material on the Treaty of Washington.

1552 FLOWER, B. O. "The Proposed Federation of the Anglo-Saxon Nations." *Arena*, XX (1898), 223−238.

1553 FOSTER, John W. "Results of the Bering Sea Arbitration." *N Am Rev*, CLXI (1895), 693−702.

1554 GARDINER, Charles A. *The Proposed Anglo-American Alliance.* New York, 1898.

1555 GARVIN, James L. *The Life of Joseph Chamberlain.* 3 vols. London, 1932−1934.

1556 GAY, James T. "The Bering Sea Controversy: Harrison, Blaine and Cronyism." *Alaska Journal*, III (1973), 12−19.

1557 GELBER, Lionel M. *The Rise of Anglo-American Friendship: A Study in World Politics, 1898−1906.* New York, 1938.

1558 GODKIN, Edwin L. "American Hatred of England." *The Nation*, LXII (1896), 46−47.

1559 HACKETT, Frank Warren. *Reminiscences of the Geneva Tribunal of Arbitration, 1872: The Alabama Claims.* Boston, 1911.

1560 HEINDEL, Richard H. *The American Impact on Great Britain, 1898−1914.* Philadelphia, 1940.

1561 HINCKLEY, T. C. "George Osgoodby and the Murchison Letter." *Pac Hist Rev*, XXVII (1958), 359−370.

1562 ISHAM, Charles. *The Fishery Question: Its Origin, History, and Present Situation.* New York, 1887.

1563 JENKINS, Brian. *Fenians and Anglo-American Relations during Reconstruction.* See **1424.**

1564 JORDAN, David S. *The Fur Seals and Fur-Seal Islands of the North Pacific Ocean.* Washington, 1898.

1565 KELLEY, Robert. *The Transatlantic Persuasion: The Liberal-Democratic Mind in the Age of Gladstone.* New York, 1969.

1566 KNAPLUND, Paul. *Gladstone and Britain's Imperial Policy.* New York, 1927.

1567 LOWELL, James Russell. "On a Certain Condescension in Foreigners." *Atl Mon*, XXIII (1869), 82−94.

1568 MARTIN, Fredericka. *The Hunting of the Silver Fleece: Epic of the Fur Seal.* New York, 1946.

1569 MILLS, David. "Which Shall Dominate—Saxon or Slav?" *N Am Rev*, CLXVI (1898), 729 – 739.

1570 MORROW, R. L. "The Negotiation of the Anglo-American Treaty of 1870." *Am Hist Rev*, XXXIX (1934), 663 – 681.

1571 MOWAT, Robert B. *The Life of Lord Pauncefote, First Ambassador to the United States.* Boston, 1929.

1572 MUNRO, John A., ed. *The Alaska Boundary Dispute.* Toronto, Can., 1970.

1573 NEALE, Robert G. *Great Britain and United States Expansion: 1898 – 1900.* East Lansing, Mich., 1966.

1574 OLNEY, Richard. "International Isolation of the United States." See **95**.

1575 PAYNE, G. H. *England: Her Treatment of America.* New York, 1931.

1576 PENLINGTON, Norman. *The Alaska Boundary Dispute: A Critical Reappraisal.* Toronto, Can., 1972.

1577 PERKINS, Bradford. *The Great Rapprochement: England and the United States, 1895 – 1914.* New York, 1968.

1578 PHELPS, Edward J. "The Behring Sea Controversy." *Harper's New Mon Mag*, LXXXII (1891), 766 – 774.

1579 REID, T. Wemyss. *Life of the Right Honourable William Edward Forster.* 2 vols. London, 1888. Material on Treaty of Washington.

1580 REUTER, B. A. *Anglo-American Relations during the Spanish-American War.* New York, 1924.

1581 ROBSON, Maureen M. "The *Alabama* Claims and the Anglo-American Reconciliation, 1865 – 1871." *Can Hist Rev*, XLII (1961), 1 – 22.

1582 ROTHSTEIN, Morton. "America in the International Rivalry for the British Wheat Market, 1860 – 1914." *Miss Val Hist Rev*, XLVII (1960), 401 – 418.

1583 SCHURZ, Carl. "The Anglo-American Friendship." *Atl Mon*, LXXXII (1898), 433 – 440.

1584 SEED, Geoffrey. "British Reactions to American Imperialism Reflected in Journals of Opinion, 1898 – 1900." *Pol Sci Q*, LXXIII (1958), 254 – 272.

1585 SEED, Geoffrey. "British Views of American Policy in the Philippines Reflected in Journals of Opinion, 1898 – 1907." *J Am Stud*, II (1968), 49 – 64.

1586 SHAPIRO, Samuel. "Problems of International Arbitration; The Halifax Fisheries Commission of 1877." *Essex Inst Hist Coll*, XCV (1959), 21 – 31.

1587 SMALLEY, G. W. *Anglo-American Memories.* London, 1912.

1588 SMITH, Goldwin. *The Treaty of Washington, 1871: A Study of Imperial History.* Ithaca, N.Y., 1941.

1589 STACEY, C. P. "Britain's Withdrawal from North America, 1864 – 1871." *Can Hist Rev*, XXXVI (1955), 185 – 198.

1590 TEMPLE, Richard. "An Anglo-American *Versus* a European Combination." *N Am Rev*, CLXVII (1898), 307 – 317.

1591 TRACY, Benjamin F. "The Behring Sea Question." *N Am Rev*, CLVI (1893), 513 – 542.

1592 WALDSTEIN, Charles. "The English-Speaking Brotherhood." *N Am Rev*, CLXVII (1898), 223 – 238.

1593 WILLIAMS, William. "Reminiscences of the Bering Sea Arbitration." *Am J Int Law*, XXXVII (1943), 562 – 584.

2. Continental Europe

1594 BINES, Joan Paller. "The United States and the European Balance of Power: 1890 – 1908." Doctoral dissertation, University of Virginia, 1976.

1595 CARROLL, Edward J. "The Foreign Relations of the United States with Tsarist Russia 1867 – 1900." Doctoral dissertation, Georgetown University, 1953.

1596 CASSEDY, James H. "Applied Microscopy and American Pork Diplomacy: Charles Wardell Stiles in Germany, 1898 – 1899." *Isis*, LXII (1971), 5 – 20.

1597 CLIFFORD, Dale. "Elihu Benjamin Washburne: An American Diplomat in Paris, 1870 – 1871." *Prologue*, II (1970), 161 – 174.

1598 DAVIS, Calvin D. *The United States and the First Hague Peace Conference.* Ithaca, N.Y., 1962.

1599 DeCONDE, Alexander. *Half Bitter, Half Sweet: An Excursion into Italian* – American History. See **137**.

1600 DUNCAN, Bingham. "Protectionism and Pork: Witelaw Reid as Diplomat, 1889 – 1891." *Ag Hist*, XXXIII (1959), 190 – 195.

1601 FEIERTAG, Sister Loretta Clare. *American Public Opinion on the Diplomatic Relations between the United States and the Papal States, 1847 – 1867.* Washington, 1933.

1602 FISK, G. M. "German – American Diplomatic and Commercial Relations Historically Considered." *Rev of Rev*, XX (1902), 323 – 328.

1603 GAZLEY, J. G. *American Opinion of German Unification, 1848 – 1871.* See **969**.

1604 GIGNILLIAT, John L. "Pigs, Politics, and Protection: The European Boycott of American Pork, 1879 – 1891." *Ag Hist*, XXXV (1961), 3 – 12.

1605 HAURY, Clifford Walter. "America and the European Balance of Power, 1866 – 1894." Doctoral dissertation, University of Virginia, 1976.

1606 HERBST, Jurgen. *The German Historical School in American Scholarship: A Study in the Transfer of Culture.* Ithaca, N.Y., 1965.

1607 HOLLS, F. W. *The Peace Conference at the Hague.* New York, 1900.

1608 HUMPHREYS, S. E. "United States Recognition of the Kingdom of Italy." *The Historian*, XXI (1959), 296 – 312.

1609 KARLIN, J. A. "The Italo-American Incident of 1891 and the Road to Reunion." *J S Hist*, VIII (1942), 242 – 246.

1610 KEIM, Jeannette L. *Forty Years of German-American Political Relations.* See **143**.

1611 McCLURE, Wallace. "German-American Commercial Relations." *Am J Int Law*, XIX (1925), 689 – 701.

1612 SCHIEBER, Clara E. *The Transformation of American Sentiment toward Germany, 1870 – 1914.* Boston, 1923.

1613 SCOTT, James Brown, ed. *The Proceedings of the Hague Peace Conferences.* 5 vols. New York, 1920 – 1921.

1614 SCOTT, James Brown. *The Hague Conventions and Declarations of 1899 and 1907.* New York, 1915.

1615 SIMON, Matthew, and David E. NOVACK. "Some Dimensions of the American Commercial Invasion of Europe, 1871–1914: An Introductory Essay." *J Econ Hist,* XXIV (1964), 591–605.

1616 SNYDER, Louis L. "The American-German Pork Dispute, 1879–1891." *J Mod Hist,* XVII (1945), 16–28.

1617 STOLBERG-WERNIGERODE, Otto zu. *Germany and the United States of America during the Era of Bismarck.* Reading, Pa., 1937.

1618 TILBERG, Frederick. *The Development of Commerce between the United States and Sweden, 1870–1925.* Moline, Ill., 1930.

1619 TRAUTH, Sister Mary Philip. *Italo-American Diplomatic Relations, 1861–1882.* See **1332**.

1620 VAGTS, Alfred. *Deutschland und die Vereinigten Staaten in der Weltpolitick, 1890–1906.* 2 vols. New York, 1935.

3. The Mediterranean and Africa

1621 CLENDENEN, Clarence C., Robert COLLINS, and Peter DUIGNAN. *Americans in Africa, 1865–1890.* Stanford, Cal., 1966.

1622 CROWE, Sybil E. *The Berlin West African Conference, 1884–1885.* London, 1942.

1623 FIELD, James A., Jr. "A Scheme in Regard to Cyrenaica." *Miss Val Hist Rev,* XLIV (1957), 445–468.

1624 HESSELTINE, William B., and Hazel C. WOLF. *The Blue and Gray on the Nile.* Chicago, 1961.

1625 KASSON, John A. "The Congo Conference and the President's Message." *N Am Rev,* CXLII (1886), 119–133.

1626 MAY, Arthur J. "Crete and the United States, 1866–1869." *J Mod Hist,* XVI (1944), 286–293.

1627 McSTALLSWORTH, Paul. "The United States and the Congo Question, 1884–1914." Doctoral dissertation, Ohio State University, 1954.

1628 NOER, Thomas John. "The United States and South Africa, 1870–1914." Doctoral dissertation, University of Minnesota, 1972.

1629 PHILLIPS, Dennis Heath. "The American Presence in Morocco, 1880–1904." Doctoral dissertation, University of Wisconsin, 1972.

1630 SANFORD, Henry S. "American Interests in Africa." *Forum,* IX (1890), 409–429.

1631 YESELSON, Abraham. *United States–Persian Diplomatic Relations, 1883–1921.* See **162**.

XI. Asia and the Pacific: 1865-1895

1. General Studies

1632 BANCROFT, Hubert Howe. *The New Pacific.* New York, 1899.

1633 BATTISTINI, Lawrence H. *The Rise of American Influence in Asia and the Pacific.* East Lansing, Mich., 1960.

1634 CLYDE, Paul H. *The Far East: A History of the Impact of the West on Eastern Asia.* Englewood Cliffs, N.J. 1958.

1635 DENNETT, Tyler. "Seward's Far Eastern Policy." *Am Hist Rev,* XXVIII (1922), 45–62.

1636 FOSTER, John W. *American Diplomacy in the Orient.* See **1029**.

1637 HUDSON, G. P. *The Far East in World Politics.* Oxford, Eng., 1937.

1638 LANGER, William L. *The Diplomacy of Imperialism.* 2 vols. New York, 1935. Mostly European.

1639 MOON, Parker T. *Imperialism and World Politics.* New York, 1926.

1640 MORSE, H. B., and H. F. McNAIR. *Far Eastern International Relations.* Boston, 1931.

1641 STEPHENS, H. Morse, and Herbert E. BOLTON. *The Pacific Ocean in History.* New York, 1917.

1642 TOMPKINS, Pauline. *American-Russian Relations in the Far East.* New York, 1949.

1643 VAN ALSTYNE, Richard W. "Myth Versus Reality in the Far Eastern Policies of the United States." *International Affairs,* XXXII (1956), 287–297.

1644 VON SCHIERBRAND, Wolf. *America, Asia and the Pacific.* New York, 1904.

2. Expansionism and Anti-Expansionism

1645 AMBROSIUS, Lloyd E. "Turner's Frontier Thesis and the Modern American Empire: A Review Essay." *Civ War Hist,* XVII (1971), 332–339.

1646 BECKER, William H. "American Manufacturers and Foreign Markets, 1870–1900: Business Historians and the 'New Economic Determinists.' " *Bus Hist Rev,* XLVII (1973), 466–481.

1647 BEISNER, Robert L. "Thirty Years before Manila: E. L. Godkin, Carl Schurz, and Anti-Imperialism in the Gilded Age." *The Historian,* XXX (1968), 561–577.

1648 BURGESS, John W. *Political Science and Comparative Constitutional Law.* 2 vols. Boston, 1890.

1649 CARPENTER, Edmund J. *The American Advance: A Study in Territorial Expansion.* New York, 1903.

1650 CLARK, Dan Elbert. "Manifest Destiny and the Pacific." *Pac Hist Rev,* I (1931), 1—17.

1651 DOZER, Donald M. "Anti-Imperialism in the United States, 1865—1895: Opposition to Annexation of Overseas Territories." Doctoral dissertation, Harvard University, 1936.

1652 DOZER, Donald M. "Anti-Imperialism during the Johnson Administration." *Pac Hist Rev,* XII (1943), 253—275.

1653 DULLES, Foster Rhea. *The Imperial Years.* New York, 1956.

1654 EBLEN, Jack Ericson. *The First and Second United States Empires: Governors and Territorial Governments, 1784—1912.* Pittsburgh, Pa., 1968.

1655 FISH, Carl Russell. *The Path of Empire.* New Haven, Conn., 1919.

1656 HOBSON, John A. *Imperialism: A Study.* Ann Arbor, Mich., 1965. Largely European.

1657 KAPLAN, Lawrence S. "Frederick Jackson Turner and Imperialism." *Social Science,* XXVII (1952), 12—16.

1658 LaFEBER, Walter. "A Note on the 'Mercantilistic Imperialism' of Alfred Thayer Mahan." *Miss Val Hist Rev,* XLVIII 674—685.

1659 MAHAN, Alfred Thayer. "The United States Looking Outward." *Atl Mon,* LXVI (1890), 816—824.

1660 MOWRY, William A. *The Territorial Growth of the United States.* New York, 1902.

1661 MULLER, Dorothea R. "Josiah Strong and American Nationalism: A Reevaluation." *J Am Hist,* LIII (1966), 487—503.

1662 NICHOLS, Jeannette P. "The United States Congress and Imperialism, 1861—1897." *J Econ Hist,* XXI (1961), 526—538.

1663 PAOLINO, Ernest N. "William Henry Seward and the Foundation of the American Empire." Doctoral dissertation, Rutgers University, 1972.

1664 PAOLINO, Ernest N. *The Foundations of the American Empire: William Henry Seward and U.S. Foreign Policy.* Ithaca, N.Y., 1973.

1665 PERKINS, Whitney T. *Denial of Empire: The United States and Its Dependencies.* Leyden, Netherlands, 1962.

1666 PLESUR, Milton. "America Looking Outward: The Years from Hayes to Harrison." *The Historian,* XXII (1960), 280—295.

1667 PLESUR, Milton. "Rumblings beneath the Surface—America's Outward Thrust, 1865—1900." *The Gilded Age, A Reappraisal.* Ed. H. Wayne Morgan. Syracuse, N.Y., 1963.*

1668 PRATT, Julius W. "Alfred Thayer Mahan." *The Marcus W. Jernegan Essays in American Historiography.* Ed. William T. Hutchinson. Chicago, 1937.

1669 PRATT, Julius W. "The Ideology of American Expansion." *Essays in Honor of William E. Dodd.* Ed. Avery Craven. Chicago, 1935.

1670 PRISCO, Salvatore, III. *John Barrett, Progressive Era Diplomat: A Study of a Commercial Expansionist, 1887—1920.* University, Ala., 1973.

1671 RADKE, August Carl. "John Tyler Morgan, an Expansionist Senator, 1877—1907." Doctoral dissertation, University of Washington, 1953. Morgan was a Democrat on the Senate Foreign Relations Committee.

1672 REED, James E. "American Foreign Policy, the Politics of Missions and Josiah Strong, 1890—1900." *Church History*, XLI (1972), 230—245.

1673 SMITH, Joe P. *The Republican Expansionists of the Early Reconstruction Era.* See **1433**.

1674 SMITH, Theodore C. "Expansion after the Civil War, 1865—1871." *Pol Sci Q*, XVI (1901), 412—436.

1675 STRONG, Josiah. *Our Country: Its Possible Future and Its Present Crisis.* New York, 1885.

1676 THOMPSON, J. A. "William Appleman Williams and the 'American Empire.' " *J Am Stud*, VII (1973), 91—104. Review article.

1677 TOMPKINS, E. Berkeley. *Anti-Imperialism in the United States: The Great Debate, 1890—1920.* Philadelphia, 1970*

1678 WHELAN, J. B. "William Henry Seward, Expansionist." Doctoral dissertation, University of Rochester, 1959.

1679 WILLIAMS, William A. "The Frontier Thesis and American Foreign Policy." *Pac Hist Rev*, XXIV (1955), 379—395.

1680 WILLIAMS, William A. *The Roots of the Modern American Empire: A Study of the Growth and Shaping of Social Consciousness in a Marketplace Society.* New York, 1969.

1681 YOUNG, Marilyn Blatt. "American Expansion, 1870—1900: The Far East." *Towards a New Past: Dissenting Essays in American History.* Ed. Barton J. Bernstein. New York, 1968.*

3. The Alaska Purchase

1682 BAILEY, Thomas A. "Why the United States Purchased Alaska." *Pac Hist Rev*, III (1934), 39—49.

1683 BANCROFT, Hubert Howe. *History of Alaska, 1730—1885.* San Francisco, Cal., 1886.

1684 BLAINE, James G. *Twenty Years of Congress: From Lincoln to Garfield.* 2 vols. Norwich, Conn., 1884—1886. Senate view of the Alaska purchase.

1685 BLODGET, Lorin. "Alaska, What Is It Worth?" *Lippincott's Magazine*, I (1868), 184—191.

1686 CALLAHAN, James M. *The Alaska Purchase and Americo-Canadian Relations.* Morgantown, W.V., 1908.

1687 CHEVIGNY, Hector. *Russian America: The Great Alaska Venture, 1741—1867.* New York, 1965.

1688 DUNNING, William A. "Paying for Alaska: Some Unfamiliar Incidents in the Process." *Pol Sci Q*, XXVII (1912), 385—398.

1689 FARRAR, Victor J. *The Annexation of Russian America to the United States.* Washington, 1937.

1690 FARRAR, Victor J. "Background to the Purchase of Alaska." *Washington Hist Q*, XIII (1922), 93 – 104.

1691 FARRAR, Victor J. "Senator Cornelius Cole and the Purchase of Alaska." *Washington Hist Q*, XIV (1923), 243 – 247.

1692 FARRAR, Victor J. "Joseph Lane MacDonald and the Purchase of Alaska." *Washington Hist Q*, XII (1921), 83 – 90.

1693 GOLDER, Frank A. "The Purchase of Alaska." *Am Hist Rev*, XXV (1920), 411 – 425.

1694 JACKSON, C. Ian. "The Stikine Territory Lease and Its Relevance to the Alaska Purchase." *Pac Hist Rev*, XXXVI (1967), 289 – 306.

1695 JENSEN, Ronald J. *The Alaska Purchase and Russian-American Relations.* Seattle, Wash., 1975.

1696 KUSHNER, Howard I. "American-Russian Rivalry in the Pacific Northwest, 1790 – 1867." Doctoral dissertation, Cornell University, 1970.

1697 LUTHIN, Reinhard H. "The Sale of Alaska." *Slavonic Rev*, XVI (1937), 168 – 182.

1698 MAZOUR, Anatole G. "The Prelude to Russia's Departure from America." See **873**.

1699 McPHERSON, Hallie M. "The Projected Purchase of Alaska, 1859 – 60." *Pac Hist Rev*, III (1934), 80 – 87.

1700 McPHERSON, Hallie M. "The Interest of William McKendree Gwin in the Purchase of Alaska, 1854 – 1861." *Pac Hist Rev*, III (1934), 28 – 38.

1701 MILLER, David Hunter, "Russian Opinion on the Cession of Alaska." *Am Hist Rev*, XLVIII (1943), 521 – 531.

1702 REID, Virginia H. *The Purchase of Alaska: Contemporary Opinion.* Long Beach Cal., 1940.

1703 SHERWOOD, Morgan B., ed. *Alaska and Its History.* Seattle, Wash., 1967.

1704 SHERWOOD, Morgan B. "George Dividson and the Acquisition of Alaska." *Pac Hist Rev*, XXVIII (1959), 141 – 154.

1705 SHIELS, Archie W. *The Purchase of Alaska.* College, Alaska, 1967.

1706 TARSAIDZE, Alexandre. *Czars and Presidents.* New York, 1958.

1707 WELCH, Richard E., Jr. "American Public Opinion and the Purchase of Russian America." *Am Slavic and E Eur Rev*, XVII (1958), 481 – 494.

4. China, Japan, and Korea

1708 ANDERSON, David Louis. "To the Open Door: America's Search for a Policy in China, 1861 – 1900." Doctoral dissertation, University of Virginia, 1974.

1709 ANGELL, James B. "The Diplomatic Relation between the United States and Japan." *J Soc Sci*, XVII (1883), 24–26.

1710 ANGELL, James B. *The Reminiscences of James Burrill Angell*. New York, 1912. A long chapter on Angell's mission to China.

1711 ATKINS, Emily H. "General Charles Legendre and the Japanese Expedition to Formosa, 1874." Doctoral dissertation, University of Florida, 1954.

1712 BANNO, Masataka. *China and the West, 1858–1861: The Origins of the Tsungli Yamen*. Cambridge, Mass., 1964.

1713 BARTH, Gunther. *Bitter Strength: A History of the Chinese in the United States, 1850–1870*. Cambridge, Mass., 1964.

1714 BIGGERSTAFF, Knight. "The Official Chinese Attitude toward the Burlingame Mission." *Am Hist Rev*, XLI (1936), 682–701.

1715 CARRANCO, Lynwood. "Chinese Expulsion from Humboldt County." *Pac Hist Rev*, XXX (1961), 329–340.

1716 CARUTHERS, Sandra. "Charles Legendre, American Diplomacy and Expansionism in Meiji Japan, 1868–1893." Doctoral dissertation, University of Colorado, 1966.

1717 CASSEY, John William. "The Mission of Charles Denby and International Rivalries in the Far East, 1885–1898." Doctoral dissertation, University of Southern California, 1959.

1718 CHIU, Ping. *Chinese Labor in California, 1850–1880: An Economic Study*. Madison, Wis., 1964.

1719 CLYDE, Paul H. "Attitudes and Policies of George F. Seward, American Minister to Peking, 1876–1880: Some Phases of the Cooperative Policy." *Pac Hist Rev*, II (1933), 387–404.

1720 COHEN, Paul. *China and Christianity: The Missionary Movement and the Growth of Chinese Antiforeignism, 1860–1870*. Cambridge, Mass., 1963.

1721 COOLIDGE, Mary R. *Chinese Immigration*. New York, 1909.

1722 CRANE, Paul. "The Chinese Massacre." *Annals of Wyoming*, XII (1940), 47–55, 153–161.

1723 DENNETT, Tyler. "Early American Policy in Korea, 1883–7: The Services of Lieutenant George C. Foulk." *Pol Sci Q*, XXXVIII (1923), 82–103.

1724 DORWART, Jeffery M. "Walter Quintin Gresham and East Asia, 1894–1895: A Reappraisal." *Asian Forum*, V (1973), 55–63.

1725 DURST, John H. "The Exclusion of the Chinese." *N Am Rev*, CXXXIX (1884), 256–273.

1726 FAIRBANK, John K. " 'American China Policy' to 1898: A Misconception." *Pac Hist Rev*, XXIX (1970), 409–420.

1727 GORDON, Leonard. "Diplomacy of the Japanese Expedition to Formosa, 1874." *Transactions of the International Conference of Orientalists in Japan*, No. 5 (1960), 48–57.

1728 GORDON, Leonard. "Formosa as an International Prize in the Nineteenth Century." Doctoral dissertation, University of Michigan, 1961.

1729 HARRINGTON, Fred H. *God, Mammon, and the Japanese: Dr. Horace N. Allen and Korean-American Relations, 1884–1905*. Madison, Wis., 1944.

1730 HSU, Immanuel C. Y. China's Entrance into the Family of Nations: The Diplomatic Phase, 1858 – 1880. Cambridge, Mass., 1960.

1731 JOSEPH, Philip. *Foreign Diplomacy in China, 1894*–1900: A Study in Political and Economic Relations with China. New York, 1971.

1732 KARLIN, J. A. "Anti-Chinese Outbreaks in Seattle, 1885 – 1866." *Pac Northwest Q*, XXXIX (1948), 103 – 130.

1733 KARLIN, J. A. "The Anti-Chinese Outbreak in Tacoma, 1885." *Pac Hist Rev*, XXIII (1954), 271 – 283.

1734 KEETON, G. W. *The Development of Extraterritorality in China.* 2 vols. London, 1928.

1735 KIM, Samuel. "America's First Minister to China: Anson Burlingame and the Tsungli Yamen." *Maryland Historian*, III (1972), 87 – 104.

1736 KNIGHT, Barry Lee. "American Trade and Investment in China, 1890 – 1910." Doctoral dissertation, Michigan State University, 1968.

1737 KUNG, S. W. *Chinese in American Life: Some Aspects of Their History, Status, Problems, and Contributions.* Seattle, Wash., 1962.

1738 LEE, Rose Hum. *The Chinese in the United States of America.* Hong Kong, 1960.

1739 LEE, Yur-Bok. *Diplomatic Relations between the United States and Korea, 1866 – 1887.* New York, 1970.

1740 LIU, Daniel T. J. "A Historical Study of Sino-American Official Relations, 1860 – 1890." *Chinese Culture*, XIV (1973), 1 – 17.

1741 MAYO, Marlene J. "A Catechism of Western Diplomacy: The Japanese and Hamilton Fish." *J Asian Stud*, XXVI (1967), 389 – 410.

1742 McCLELLAN, Robert. *The Heathen Chinese: A Study of American Attitudes toward China, 1890 – 1905.* Columbus, Ohio, 1971.

1743 McCUNE, George M., and John A. HARRISON, eds. *Korean-American Relations: Documents Pertaining to the Far Eastern Diplomacy of the United States.* Vol. I: *The Initial Period, 1883 – 1886.* Berkeley, Cal., 1951.

1744 MILLER, Stuart C. *The Unwelcome Immigrant: The American Image of the Chinese, 1785 – 1882.* Berkeley, Cal., 1969.

1745 NELSON, Melvin Frederick. *Korea and the Old Orders in Eastern Asia.* Baton Rouge, La., 1945.

1746 NEU, Charles E. *The Troubled Encounter: The United States and Japan.* New York, 1975.

1747 NEUMANN, William L. "Determinism, Destiny, and Myth in the American Image of China." *Issues and Conflicts.* Ed. George L. Anderson. Lawrence, Kans., 1959.

1748 NITOBE, Inazo. *The Intercourse between the United States and Japan.* Baltimore, 1891.

1749 NOBLE, Harold J. "The United States and Sino-Korean Relations, 1885 – 1887." *Pac Hist Rev*, II (1933), 292 – 304.

1750 OSBORN, Clarence G. *American Extraterritorial Jurisdiction in China to 1906: A Study of American Policy.* Stanford, Cal., 1935.

1751 PALMER, Spencer J., ed. *Korean-American Relations: Documents Pertaining to the Far Eastern Diplomacy of the United States.* Vol. II: *The Period of Growing Influence, 1887– 1895.* Berkeley, Cal., 1963.

1752 PAUL, Rodman W. "The Origins of the Chinese Issue in California." *Miss Val Hist Rev,* XXV (1938), 181 – 196.

1753 PAULLIN, Charles O. "The Opening of Korea by Commodore Shufeldt." *Pol Sci Q,* XXV (1910), 470 – 499.

1754 PAULSEN, G. E. "The Gresham-Yang Treaty [1894]. *Pac Hist Rev,* XXXVII (1968), 281 – 297.

1755 PELCOVITS, Nathan Albert. *Old China Hands and the Foreign Office.* New York, 1948.

1756 PRICE, Allen T. "American Missions and American Diplomacy in China, 1830 – 1900." Doctoral dissertation, Harvard University, 1932.

1757 PURCELL, Victor. *The Boxer Uprising: A Background Study.* Cambridge, Eng., 1963.

1758 SANDMEYER, Elmer C. *The Anti-Chinese Movement in California.* Urbana, Ill., 1939.

1759 SEAGER, Robert, II. "Some Denominational Reactions to Chinese Immigration to California, 1856 – 1892." *Pac Hist Rev,* XXVIII (1959), 49 – 66.

1760 SEWARD, George F. *Chinese Immigration, in Its Social and Economical Aspects.* New York, 1881.

1761 SEWARD, George F. "Mongolian Immigration." *N Am Rev,* CXXXIV (1882), 562 – 577.

1762 SMITH, Shirley W. *James Burrill Angell: An American Influence.* Ann Arbor, Mich., 1954.

1763 SPEER, William. *The Oldest and the Newest Empire: China and the United States.* Cincinnati, Ohio, 1870.

1764 TATE, E. Mowbray. "U.S. Gunboats on the Yangtze: History and Political Aspects, 1842 – 1922." *Studies on Asia,* VII (1966), 121 – 132.

1765 TREAT, Payson J. *Diplomatic Relations between the United States and Japan, 1853– 1905.* See **1053**.

1766 TREAT, Payson J. "The Good Offices of the United States during the Sino-Japanese War. *Pol Sci Q,* XLVII (1932), 547 – 555.

1767 TSIANG, I-Mieng. *The Question of Expatriation in America Prior to 1907.* Baltimore, 1942.

1768 VARG, Paul A. *Missionaries, Chinese, and Diplomats: The American Protestant Missionary Movement in China, 1890– 1952.* See **193**.

1769 WILLIAMS, F. W. *Anson Burlingame and the First Chinese Mission to Foreign Powers.* New York, 1912.

1770 WILLIAMS, S. Wells. *The Middle Kingdom: A Survey of Geography, Government, Literature, Social Life, Arts, and History of the Chinese Empire and Its Inhabitants.* 2 vols. New York, 1883.

1771 ZABRISKIE, Edward H. *American-Russian Rivalry in the Far East: A Study in Diplomacy and Power Politics, 1895– 1914.* Philadelphia, Pa., 1946.

5. The Pacific Islands

1772 ADLER, Jacob. *Claus Spreckels: The Sugar King in Hawaii.* Honolulu, 1966.

1773 ADLER, Jacob. "The Oceanic Steamship Company: A Link in Claus Spreckels' Hawaiian Sugar Empire." *Pac Hist Rev,* XXIX (1960), 257—269.

1774 ALEXANDER, William D. *History of Later Years of the Hawaiian Monarchy and the Revolution of 1893.* Honolulu, 1896.

1775 APPEL, John C. "American Labor and the Annexation of Hawaii: A Study in Logic and Economic Interest." *Pac Hist Rev,* XXIII (1954), 1—18.

1776 BAILEY, Thomas A. "Japan's Protest Against the Annexation of Hawaii." *J Mod Hist,* III (1931), 46—51.

1777 BAILEY, Thomas A. "The United States and Hawaii During the Spanish-American War." *Am Hist Rev,* XXXVI (1931), 552—560.

1778 BAKER, George W. "Benjamin Harrison and Hawaiian Annexation: A Reinterpretation." *Pac Hist Rev,* XXXIII (1964), 295—309.

1779 BISHOP, Sereno E. "The Hawaiian Queen and Her Kingdom." *Rev of Rev,* IV (1891), 147—163.

1780 BRYCE, James. "The Policy of Annexation for America." *Forum,* XXIV (1897), 385—395.

1781 CONROY, Francis H. *The Japanese Frontier in Hawaii, 1868—1898.* Berkeley, Cal., 1953.

1782 DAMON, Ethel M. *Sanford Ballard Dole and His Hawaii.* Stanford, Cal., 1957.

1783 DOLE, Sanford B. *Memoirs of the Hawaiian Revolution.* Ed. Andrew Farrell. Honolulu, 1936.

1784 DOZER, Donald M. "The Opposition to Hawaiian Reciprocity, 1876-1888." *Pac Hist Rev,* XIV (1945), 157—183.

1785 ELLISON, Joseph W. "The Partition of Samoa: A Study in Imperialism and Diplomacy." *Pac Hist Rev,* VIII (1939), 259—288.

1786 ELLISON, Joseph W. "The Adventures of an American Premier in Samoa, 1874—1876." *Pac Northwest Q,* XXVII (1936), 311—346.

1787 GILSON, Richard P. *Samoa, 1830—1900: The Politics of a Multi-Cultural Community.* Melbourne, 1970.

1788 GRAY, J. A. C. "The Apia Hurricane of 1889." *Proc US Naval Inst,* LXXXVI (1960), 34—39.

1789 KENNEDY, Paul M. *The Samoan Tangle: A Study in Anglo-German-American Relations, 1878—1900.* New York, 1974.

1790 KUYKENDALL, Ralph Simpson. *The Hawaiian Kingdom, 1854—1874.* See **1038**.

1791 KUYKENDALL, Ralph Simpson. *The Hawaiian Kingdom, 1874-1893: The Kalakaua Dynasty.* Honolulu, 1938.

1792 LANIER, Osmos, Jr. " 'Paramount' Blount: Special Commissioner to Investigate the Hawaiian *Coup, 1893.*" *West Georgia College Studies in the Social Sciences,* XI (1972), 45—55.

1793 LILIUOKALANI, Queen. *Hawaii's Story by Hawaii's Queen.* Boston, 1898.

1794 LODGE, Henry Cabot. "Our Blundering Foreign Policy." *Forum,* XIX (1895), 8—17.

1795 MAHAN, Alfred Thayer, "Hawaii and Our Future Sea-Power." *Forum,* XV (1893), 1—11.

1796 MASTERMAN, Sylvia. *The Origins of International Rivalry in Samoa, 1845—1884.* Stanford, Cal., 1934.

1797 McINTYRE, W. D. "Anglo-American Rivalry in the Pacific: The British Annexation of the Fiji Islands in 1874." *Pac Hist Rev,* XXIX (1960), 361—380.

1798 MORGAN, John T. "The Duty of Annexing Hawaii." *Forum,* XXV (1898), 11—16.

1799 PATTERSON, John. "The United States and Hawaiian Reciprocity, 1867—1870." *Pac Hist Rev,* VII (1938), 14—26.

1800 PENFIELD, Walter S. "The Settlement of the Samoan Cases." *Am J Int Law,* VII (1913), 767—773.

1801 PRATT, Julius W. "The Hawaiian Revolution: A New Interpretation." *Pac Hist Rev,* I (1932), 273—294.

1802 PROCTER, John R. "Hawaii and the Changing Front of the World." Forum, XXIV (1897), 34—45.

1803 ROLLE, A. F. "California Filibustering and the Hawaiian Kingdom." *Pac Hist Rev,* XIX (1950), 251—263.

1804 ROWLAND, Donald W. "The United States and the Contract Labor Question in Hawaii, 1862—1900." *Pac Hist Rev,* II (1933), 249—269.

1805 RUSS, William A., Jr. "Hawaiian Labor and Immigration Problems before Annexation." *J Mod Hist,* XV (1943), 207—222.

1806 RUSS, William A., Jr. *The Hawaiian Republic, 1894—98.* Selinsgrove, Pa., 1961.

1807 RUSS, William A., Jr. *The Hawaiian Revolution, 1893—94.* Selinsgrove, Pa., 1959.

1808 RUSS, William A., Jr. "The Role of Sugar in Hawaiian Annexation." *Pac Hist Rev,* XII (1943), 339—350.

1809 RYDEN, George H. *The Foreign Policy of the United States in Relation to Samoa.* New Haven, Conn., 1933.

1810 SPRECKELS, Claus. "The Future of the Sandwich Islands." *N Am Rev,* CLII (1891), 287—291.

1811 STEVENS, John L. "A Plea for Annexation." *N Am Rev,* CLVII (1893), 736—745.

1812 STEVENS, Sylvester K. *American Expansion in Hawaii, 1842—1898.* Harrisburg, Pa., 1945.

1813 STEVENSON, Robert Louis. *A Foot-Note to History: Eight Years of Trouble in Samoa.* New York, 1897.

1814 TANSILL, Charles C. *Diplomatic Relations Between the United States and Hawaii, 1885—1889.* New York, 1940.

1815 TATE, Merze. "British Opposition to the Cession of Pearl Harbor." *Pac Hist Rev*, XXIX (1960), 381 – 394.

1816 TATE, Merze. "Canada's Interest in the Trade and Sovereignty of Hawaii." *Can Hist Rev*, XLIV (1963), 20 – 42.

1817 TATE, Merze. "Hawaii: A Symbol of Anglo-American Rapprochment." *Pol Sci Q*, LXXIX (1964), 555 – 575.

1818 TATE, Merze. *Hawaii: Reciprocity or Annexation.* East Lansing, Mich., 1968.

1819 TATE, Merze. "The Myth of Hawaii's Swing toward Australasia and Canada." *Pac Hist Rev*, XXXIII (1964), 273 – 293.

1820 TATE, Merze. "Slavery and Racism as Deterrents to the Annexation of Hawaii, 1854 – 1855." See **1051**.

1821 TATE, Merze. "Twisting the Lion's Tail over Hawaii." *Pac Hist Rev*, XXXVI (1967), 27 – 46.

1822 TATE, Merze. *The United States and the Hawaiian Kingdom: A Political History.* New Haven, Conn., 1965.

1823 THURSTON, Lorrin A. *Memoirs of the Hawaiian Revolution.* Ed. Andrew Farrell. Honolulu, 1936.

1824 THURSTON, Lorrin A. "The Sandwich Islands: I. The Advantages of Annexation." *N Am Rev*, CLVI (1893), 265 – 281.

1825 WAKEMAN, Edgar. *Report of Capt. E. Wakeman, to W. H. Webb, on the Islands of the Samoa Group.* New York, 1872.

1826 WEIGLE, Richard D. "Sugar and the Hawaiian Revolution." *Pac Hist Rev*, XVI (1947), 41 – 58.

1827 YOUNG, Lucien. *The Boston at Hawaii.* Washington, 1898.

6. Strategy and Foreign Policy

1828 BRAISTED, William R. *The United States Navy in the Pacific, 1897 – 1909.* Austin, Tex., 1958.

1829 CHALLENER, Richard D. *Admirals, Generals, and American Foreign Policy, 1898 – 1914.* Princeton, N.J., 1973.

1830 DAVIS, George T. *A Navy Second to None: The Development of Modern American Naval Policy.* New York, 1940.

1831 GRENVILLE, John A. S. "Diplomacy and War Plans in the United States, 1890 – 1917." *Trans Royal Hist Soc*, XI (1961), 1 – 21.

1832 GRENVILLE, John A. S., and George Berkeley YOUNG. *Politics, Strategy and American Diplomacy: Studies in Foreign Policy, 1873 – 1917.* See **275**.

1833 HAGAN, Kenneth J. *American Gunboat Diplomacy and the Old Navy, 1877 – 1889.* Westport, Conn., 1973.

1834 HERRICK, Walter R., Jr. *The American Naval Revolution.* Baton Rouge, La., 1966.

1835 KARSTEN, Peter. *The Naval Aristocracy: The Golden Age of Annapolis and the Emergence of Modern American Navalism.* New York, 1972. Focuses on the late nineteenth century.

1836 LIVERMORE, Seward W. "American Naval-Base Policy in the Far East, 1850–1914." *Pac Hist Rev*, XIII (1944), 113–135.

1837 LIVEZEY, William E. *Mahan on Sea Power.* See **278**.

1838 MAHAN, Alfred Thayer. *The Interest of America in Sea Power, Present and Future.* Boston, 1898.

1839 MAHAN, Alfred Thayer. "The Isthmus and Sea Power." *Atl Mon*, LXXII (1893), 459–472.

1840 MAHAN, Alfred Thayer. "Possibilities of an Anglo-American Reunion." *N Am Rev*, CLIX (1894), 551–563.

1841 MAHAN, Alfred Thayer. "Preparedness for Naval War." *Harper's New Mon Mag*, XCIV (1897), 579–588.

1842 MITCHELL, Donald W. *History of the Modern American Navy, from 1883 through Pearl Harbor.* New York, 1946.

1843 PAULLIN, Charles O. *Diplomatic Negotiations of American Naval Officers, 1778–1883.* Baltimore, 1912.

1844 PAULLIN, Charles O. "A Half Century of Naval Administration in America, 1861–1911." *Proc US Naval Inst*, XXXVIII (1912).

1845 POMEROY, Earl S. *Pacific Outpost: American Strategy in Guam and Micronesia.* See **185**.

1846 PULESTON, William D. *Mahan: The Life and Work of Captain Alfred Thayer Mahan, U.S.N.* New Haven, Conn., 1939.

1847 SEAGER, Robert, II. "Ten Years before Mahan: The Unofficial Case for the New Navy, 1880–1890." *Miss Val Hist Rev*, XL (1953), 491–512.

1848 SPEARS, John R. *The History of Our Navy: From Its Origin to the End of the War with Spain, 1775–1898.* 5 vols. New York, 1902.

1849 SPROUT, Harold, and Margaret SPROUT. *The Rise of American Naval Power, 1776–1918.* Princeton, N.J., 1939.

1850 WEST, Richard S., Jr. *Admirals of American Empire: The Combined Story of George Dewey, Alfred Thayer Mahan, Winfield Scott Schley, and William Thomas Sampson.* Indianapolis, 1948.

XII. World Power: The McKinley Years

1. General Studies

1851 ALLEN, Gardner W., ed. *Papers of John Davis Long, 1897–1904.* Boston, 1939.

1852 BAILEY, Thomas A. "America's Emergence as a World Power: The Myth and the Verity." See **55**.

1853 BAILEY, Thomas A. "Was the Election of 1900 a Mandate on Imperialism?" *Miss Val Hist Rev*, XXIV (1937), 43–52.

1854 BEALE, Howard K. *Theodore Roosevelt and the Rise of America to World Power*. Baltimore, 1956.*

1855 BOWERS, Claude G. *Beveridge and the Progressive Era*. New York, 1932.

1856 BURTON, David Henry. *Theodore Roosevelt: Confident Imperialist*. Philadelphia, 1969.

1857 BUSSELLE, James Arthur. "The United States in the Far East, 1894–1905: The Years of Illusion." Doctoral dissertation, University of Virginia, 1975.

1858 CAMPBELL, Alexander E., ed. *Expansion and Imperialism*. New York, 1970.

1859 CLEMENTS, Kendrick Alling. "William Jennings Bryan and Democratic Foreign Policy, 1896-1915." Doctoral dissertation, University of California, Berkeley, 1970.

1860 CLYMER, Kenton J. *John Hay: The Gentleman as Diplomat*. Ann Arbor, Mich., 1975.

1861 COLETTA, Paola E., ed. *Threshold to American Internationalism: Essays on the Foreign Policies of William McKinley*. New York, 1970.

1862 COLETTA, Paola E. "William McKinley and the Conduct of United States Foreign Relations." *Threshold to American Internationalism*. See **1861**.

1863 COOLIDGE, Archibald Cary. *The United States as a World Power*. New York, 1908.

1864 COY, Dwight Richard. "Cushman K. Davis and American Foreign Policy, 1887–1900." Doctoral dissertation, University of Minnesota, 1965. Davis was chairman of the Senate Foreign Relations Committee.

1865 DAWES, Charles G. *A Journal of the McKinley Years, Edited, and with a Foreword, by Bascom N. Timmons*. Chicago, 1950.

1866 DENNETT, Tyler. *John Hay: From Poetry to Politics*. New York, 1933.

1867 DENNIS, A. L. P. *Adventures in American Diplomacy, 1896–1906*. New York, 1928.

1868 DULLES, Foster Rhea. *America's Rise to World Power*. New York, 1955.

1869 DULLES, Foster Rhea. "John Hay." *An Uncertain Tradition: American Secretaries of State in the Twentieth Century*. Ed. Norman A. Graebner. New York, 1961.*

1870 FAULKNER, Harold U. *Politics, Reform, and Expansion, 1890–1900*. New York, 1959.

1871 FONER, Philip S. *The Spanish-Cuban-American War and the Birth of American Imperialism*, 1895–1902. 2 vols. New York, 1972.

1872 GARRATY, John A. *Henry Cabot Lodge: A Biography*. New York, 1953.

1873 GATEWOOD, Willard B., Jr. "Black Americans and the Quest for Empire, 1898–1903." *J S Hist*, XXXVIII (1972), 545–566.

1874 GATEWOOD, Willard B., Jr. "A Negro Editor on Imperialism: John Mitchell, 1898–1901." *Jour Q*, XLIX (1972), 43–50.

1875 GRISWOLD, A. Whitney. *The Far Eastern Policy of the United States*. New York, 1938.*

1876 HARRISON, Benjamin Taylor. "Chandler Anderson and American Foreign Relations (1896—1928)." Doctoral dissertation, University of California, Los Angeles, 1969. Anderson was an international lawyer and consultant to the State Department.

1877 HAY, John. *Letters of John Hay and Extracts from Diary*. 3 vols. Washington, 1908.

1878 HEALY, David F. *US Expansionism: The Imperialist Urge in the 1890s*. Madison, Wis., 1970.

1879 HOFSTADTER, Richard. "Cuba, the Philippines, and Manifest Destiny." *America in Crisis*. Ed. Daniel Aaron. New York, 1952.

1880 HOFSTADTER, Richard. *The Paranoid Style in American Politics, and Other Essays*. New York, 1965.

1881 HOLBO, Paul S. "Perspectives on American Foreign Policy, 1890—1916: Expansion and World Power." *Soc Stud*, LVIII (1967), 246—256. A bibliographical essay.

1882 IRIYE, Akira. *Across the Pacific: An Inner History of American—East Asian Relations*. New York, 1967.

1883 IRIYE, Akira. *Pacific Estrangement: Japanese and American Expansion, 1897—1911*. Cambridge, Mass., 1972.

1884 KENNAN, George F. *American Diplomacy, 1900—1950*. See **86**.

1885 KENNEDY, P. C. "La Follette's Imperialist Flirtation." *Pac Hist Rev*, XXIX (1960), 131—144.

1886 KENNEDY, Philip W. "Race and American Expansion in Cuba and Puerto Rico, 1895—1905." *J Black Stud*, I (1971), 306—316.

1887 KENNEDY, Philip W. "The Racial Overtones of Imperialism as a Campaign Issue, 1900." *Mid-Am*, XLVIII (1966), 196—205.

1888 KOHLSAAT, H. H. *From McKinley to Harding*. New York, 1923.

1889 LATANE, John H. *America as a World Power, 1897—1907*. New York, 1907.

1890 LEECH, Margaret. *In the Days of McKinley*. New York, 1959.

1891 LEOPOLD, Richard W. "The Emergence of America as a World Power: Some Second Thoughts." *Change and Continuity in Twentieth-Century America*. Eds. John Braeman, Robert H. Bremner, and Everett Walters. Columbus, Ohio, 1964. A review essay.

1892 LEUCHTENBURG, William E. "Progressivism and Imperialism: The Progressive Movement and American Foreign Policy, 1898—1916." *Miss Val Hist Rev*, XXXIX (1952), 483—504.

1893 LODGE, Henry Cabot, ed. *Selections from the Correspondence of Theodore Roosevelt and Henry Cabot Lodge*. 2 vols. New York, 1925.

1894 MAY, Ernest R. *American Imperialism: A Speculative Essay*. New York, 1968.

1895 MAY, Ernest R. "Emergence to World Power." *The Reconstruction of American History*. Ed. John Higham. New York, 1962.*

1896 MAY, Ernest R. *Imperial Democracy: The Emergence of America as a Great Power.* New York, 1961.

1897 McKEE, Delber Lee. "Samuel Gompers, the A. F. of L., and Imperialism, 1895–1900." *The Historian,* XXI (1959), 187–199.

1898 MILLER, Richard H. *American Imperialism in 1898: The Quest for National Fulfillment.* New York, 1970.

1899 MORGAN, H. Wayne. *America's Road to Empire: The War with Spain and Overseas Expansion.* New York, 1965.*

1900 MORGAN, H. Wayne. *William McKinley and His America.* Syracuse, N.Y., 1963.

1901 MORISON, Elting E., *et al,* eds. *The Letters of Theodore Roosevelt.* 8 vols. Cambridge, Mass., 1951–1954.

1902 OLCOTT, Charles S. *The Life of William McKinley.* 2 vols. New York, 1916.

1903 OSGOOD, Robert E. *Ideals and Self Interest in America's Foreign Relations.* Chicago, 1953.

1904 PECK, Harry T. *Twenty Years of the Republic, 1885–1905.* New York, 1906. Work by an intelligent observer.

1905 PRATT, Julius W. *Expansionists of 1898: The Acquisition of Hawaii and the Spanish Islands.* Baltimore, 1936.*

1906 PRATT, Julius W. *America's Colonial Experiment: How the United States Gained, Governed, and in Part Gave Away a Colonial Empire.* New York, 1950.

1907 PRATT, Julius W. "The 'Large Policy' of 1898." *Miss Val Hist Rev,* XIX (1932), 219–242.

1908 REID, Whitelaw. *Problems of Expansion.* New York, 1900.

1909 RHODES, James Ford. *The McKinley and Roosevelt Administrations, 1897–1909.* New York, 1922.

1910 SWANBERG, W. A. *Citizen Hearst: A Biography of William Randolph Hearst.* New York, 1961.

1911 THAYER, William R. *The Life and Letters of John Hay.* 2 vols. Boston, 1915.

1912 TWETON, D. J. "Imperialism versus Prosperity in the Election of 1900." *North Dakota Q,* XXX (1962), 50–55.

1913 VEVIER, Charles. "Brooks Adams and the Ambivalence of American Foreign Policy." *World Aff Q,* XXX (1959), 3–18.

1914 WELCH, Richard E., Jr. *George Frisbie Hoar and the Half-Breed Republicans.* Cambridge, Mass., 1971.

1915 WILLIAMS, William A. "Brooks Adams and American Expansion." *N Eng Q,* XXV (1952), 217–232.

1916 WINKLER, John K. *W. R. Hearst: An American Phenomenon.* New York, 1928.

1917 WINKLER, John K. *William Randolph Hearst: A New Appraisal.* New York, 1955.

1918 ZABRISKIE, Edward H. *American-Russian Rivalry in the Far East, 1895–1914.* See **1771**.

2. Cuba and the Spanish American War

1919 ADAMS, Brooks. "The Spanish War and the Equilibrium of the World." *Forum*, XXV (1898), 641—651.

1920 ALGER, Russell A. *The Spanish-American War*. New York, 1901. By McKinley's Secretary of War.

1921 APPEL, John C. "The Unionization of Florida Cigarmakers and the Coming of the War with Spain." *His Am Hist Rev*, XXXVI (1956), 38—49.

1922 AUXIER, George W. "The Cuban Question As Reflected in the Editorial Columns of Middle Western Newspapers." Doctoral dissertation, Ohio State University, 1938.

1923 AUXIER, George W. "Middle Western Newspapers and the Spanish-American War, 1895—1898." *Miss Val Hist Rev*, XXVI (1940), 523—534.

1924 AUXIER, George W. "The Propaganda Activities of the Cuban *Junta* in Precipitating the Spanish American War, 1895—1898." *His Am Hist Rev*, XIX (1939), 286—305.

1925 BENTON, Elbert J. *The International Law and Diplomacy of the Spanish-American War*. Baltimore, 1908.

1926 CHADWICK, French Ensor. *The Relations of the United States and Spain: The Spanish-American War*. 2 vols. New York, 1911.

1927 DALLEK, Robert, ed. *1898: McKinley's Decision: War with Spain*. New York, 1969.

1928 EGGERT, Gerald G. "Our Man in Havana: Fitzhugh Lee." *His Am Hist Rev*, XLVII (1967), 463—485.

1929 ELLIS, Elmer. *Henry Moore Teller*. Caldwell, Idaho, 1941.

1930 FERRARA, Orestes. *The Last Spanish War: Revelations in "Diplomacy."* New York, 1937.

1931 FLACK, Horace E. *Spanish-American Diplomatic Relations Preceding the War of 1898*. Baltimore, 1906.

1932 FONER, Philip S. "The United States Went to War with Spain in 1898." *Sci Soc*, XXXII (1968), 39—65.

1933 FREIDEL, Frank. *The Splendid Little War*. New York, 1958.

1934 GILMORE, N. Ray. "Mexico and the Spanish-American War." *His Am Hist Rev*, XLIII (1963), 511—525.

1935 GRENVILLE, John A. S. "American Naval Preparations for War with Spain, 1896—1898." *J Am Stud*, II (1968), 33—47.

1936 HEALY, David F. *The United States and Cuba, 1898—1902: Generals, Politicians, and the Search for Policy*. Madison, Wis., 1963.

1937 HERSHEY, Amos S. "The Recognition of Cuban Belligerency." *Ann Am Acad of Pol Soc Sci*, VII (1896), 450—461.

1938 HOLBO, Paul S. "The Convergence of Moods and the Cuban-Bond 'Conspiracy' of 1898." *J Am Hist*, LV (1968), 54—72.

1939 HOLBO, Paul S. "Presidential Leadership in Foreign Affairs: William McKinley and the Turpie-Foraker Amendment." *Am Hist Rev*, LXXII (1967), 1321—1335.

1940 JOHNSTON, William Andrew. *History Up To Date: A Concise Account of the War of 1898 Between the United States and Spain, Its Causes and the Treaty of Paris.* New York, 1899.

1941 LaFEBER, Walter. "That 'Splendid Little War' in Historical perspective." *Tex Q*, II (1968), 89—98.

1942 Linderman, gerald F. *The Mirror of War: American Society and the Spanish-American War.* Ann Arbor, Mich., 1974.

1943 LODGE, Henry Cabot. "Our Duty to Cuba." *Forum*, XXI (1896), 278—287.

1944 LODGE, Henry Cabot. *The War with Spain.* New York, 1899.

1945 McCORMICK, Thomas J. "Insular Imperialism and the Open Door: The China Market and the Spanish-American War." *Pac Hist Rev*, XXXII (1963), 155—169.

1946 MILLIS, Walter. *The Martial Spirit: A Study of Our War with Spain.* Boston, 1931.

1947 MOORE, John Bassett. "The Question of Cuban Belligerency." *Forum*, XXI (1896), 288—300.

1948 MORGAN, H. Wayne. "The DeLome Letter: A New Appraisal." *The Historian*, XXVI (1963), 36—49.

1949 NEALE, Robert G. "Anglo-American Relations During the Spanish-American War: Some Problems." *Hist Stud Australia and New Zealand*, VI (1953), 72—89.

1950 O'CONNOR, Nancy L. "The Spanish-American War: A Re-Evaluation of Its Causes." *Sci Soc*, XXII (1958), 129—143.

1951 OFFNER, John L. "President McKinley and the Origins of the Spanish-American War." Doctoral dissertation, Pennsylvania State University, 1957.

1952 PRATT, Julius, W. "American Business and the Spanish American War." *His Am Hist Rev*, XIV (1934), 163—201.

1953 PRITCHETT, Henry S. "Some Recollections of President McKinley and the Cuban Intervention." *N Am Rev*, CLXXXIX (1909), 397—403.

1954 QUINT, Howard H. "American Socialists and the Spanish-American War." *Am Q*, X (1958), 131—141.

1955 REUTER, B. A. *Anglo-American Relations During the Spanish-American War.* New York, 1924.

1956 SHANKMAN, Arnold M. "Southern Methodist Newspapers and the Coming of the Spanish-American War: A Research Note." *J S Hist*, XXXIX (1973), 93—96.

1957 SHELBY, C. C. "Mexico and the Spanish-American War: Some Contemporary Expressions of Opinion." *Essays in Mexican History.* See **1178**.

1958 SHIPPEE, Lester B. "Germany and the Spanish-American War." *Am Hist Rev*, XXX (1925), 754—777.

1959 SKLAR, Martin J. "The NAM on the Eve of the Spanish-American War." *Sci Soc*, XXIII (1959), 133—162.

1960 WEEMS, John E. *The Fate of the Maine.* New York, 1958.

1961 WILKERSON, Marcus M. *Public Opinion and the Spanish American War: A Study in War Propaganda.* Baton Rouge, La., 1932.

1962 WILSON, H. W. *The Downfall of Spain: Naval History of the Spanish-American War.* London, 1900.

1963 WISAN, Joseph E. *The Cuban Crisis as Reflected in the New York Press, 1895–1898.* New York, 1934.

3. Puerto Rico and the Philippines

1964 BAILEY, Thomas A. "Dewey and the Germans at Manila Bay." *Am Hist Rev,* XLV (1939), 59–81.

1965 BERBUSSE, Edward J. *The United States and Puerto Rico, 1898–1900.* Chapel Hill, N.C., 1966.

1966 BLOUNT, James H. *The American Occupation of the Philippines, 1898–1912.* New York, 1912.

1967 BRAISTED, William R. "The Philippine Naval Base Problem, 1898-1909." *Miss Val Hist Rev,* XLI (1954), 21–40.

1968 BRAISTED, William R. *The United States Navy in the Pacific, 1897–1909.* See **1828**.

1969 COLETTA, Paolo E. "Bryan, McKinley, and the Treaty of Paris." *Pac Hist Rev,* XXVI (1957), 131–146.

1970 COLETTA, Paolo E. "McKinley, the Peace Negotiations, and the Acquisition of the Philippines." *Pac Hist Rev,* XXX (1961), 341–350.

1971 DENBY, Charles. "Shall We Keep the Philippines?" *Forum,* XXVI (1898), 279–281.

1972 DEWEY, George. *Autobiography of George Dewey.* New York, 1913.

1973 EYRE, James K., Jr. "Japan and the American Annexation of the Philippines." *Pac Hist Rev,* XI (1942), 55–71.

1974 EYRE, James K., Jr. "Russia and the American Acquisition of the Philippines." *Miss Val Hist Rev,* XXVIII (1942), 539–562.

1975 FORBES, William C. *The Philippine Islands.* 2 vols. Boston, 1928.

1976 FOREMAN, John. "Spain and the Philippine Islands." *Contemporary Rev,* LXXIV (1898), 20–33.

1977 GRAFF, Henry F., ed. *American Imperialism and the Philippine Insurrection.* Boston, 1969.

1978 GREENBERG, A. A. "Public Opinion and the Acquisition of the Philippine Islands. Masters thesis, Yale University, 1937.

1979 GRUNDER, Garel A., and William E. LIVEZEY. *The Philippines and the United States, 1898–1950.* See **176**.

1980 HEALY, Laurin, and Luis KUTNER. *The Admiral.* Chicago, 1944. Study of George Dewey.

1981 HOLLINGSWORTH, J. Rogers, ed. *American Expansion in the Late Nineteenth Century.* New York, 1968.

1982 KNOLES, George H., ed. "Grover Cleveland on Imperialism." *Miss Val Hist Rev*, XXXVII (1950), 303–304. A letter dated November 9, 1898.

1983 LE ROY, James A. *The Americans in the Philippines.* 2 vols. Boston, 1914.

1984 MELVILLE, George W. "Our Future on the Pacific—What We Have There to Hold and Win." *N Am Rev*, CLXVI (1898), 281–296.

1985 MORGAN, H. Wayne, ed. *Making Peace with Spain: The Diary of Whitelaw Reid, September–December, 1898.* Austin, Tex., 1965.

1986 NEALE, Robert G. *Great Britain and United States Expansion: 1898–1900.* See **1573**.

1987 PECK, Harry T. "A Spirited Foreign Policy." *Bookman*, XXI (1905), 369–379.

1988 POMEROY, William J. "Pacification in the Philippines, 1898–1913." *France Asie/Asia*, XXI (1967), 427–446.

1989 QUINN, Pearle E. "The Diplomatic Struggle for the Carolines, 1898." *Pac Hist Rev*, XIV (1945), 290–302.

1990 ROBINSON, Edward Van Dyke. "The Caroline Islands and the Terms of Peace." *Independent*, L (1898), 1046–1048.

1991 SCHURMAN, Jacob G. *Philippine Affairs, Retrospect and Prospect.* New York, 1902.

1992 SEED, Geoffrey. "British Views of American Policy in the Philippines Reflected in Journals of Opinion, 1898–1907." See **1585**.

1993 SPECTOR, Ronald. "Who Planned the Attack on Manila Bay?" *Mid-Am*, LIII (1971), 94–104.

1994 STANLEY, Peter W. *A Nation in the Making: The Philippines and the United States, 1899–1921.* Cambridge, Mass., 1974.

1995 WALKER, Leslie W. "Guam's Seizure by the United States in 1898." *Pac Hist Rev*, XIV (1945), 1–12.

1996 WELCH, Richard E., Jr. "The Philippine Insurrection and the American Press." *The Historian*, XXXVI (1973), 34–51.

1997 WILDMAN, Edwin. "What Dewey Feared in Manila Bay, as Revealed by His Letters." *Forum*, LIX (1918), 513–535.

1998 WOLFF, Leon, *Little Brown Brother: How the United States Purchased and Pacified the Philippine Islands at the Century's Turn.* Garden City, N.Y., 1961.

1999 WORCESTER, Dean C., and Hayden RALSTON. *The Philippines, Past and Present.* New York, 1930.

4. Anti-Imperialism: 1898–1899

2000 BARON, Harold. "Anti-Imperialism and the Democrats." *Sci Soc*, XXI (1957), 222–239.

2001 BEISNER, Robert L. "The Anti-Imperialist Impulse: The Mugwumps and the Republicans, 1898–1900." Doctoral dissertation, University of Chicago, 1965.

2002 BEISNER, Robert L. *Twelve Against Empire: The Anti-Imperialists, 1898–1900.* New York, 1968.

2003 BEISNER, Robert L. "1898 and 1968: The Anti-Imperialists and the Doves." *Pol Sci Q*, LXXXV (1970), 187–216.

2004 BRANTLEY, W. G. *What is to be Done with the Philippines?* Washington, 1900.

2005 BROWN, Robert Craig. "Goldwin Smith and Anti-Imperialism." *Can Hist Rev*, XLIII (1962), 93–105.

2006 CARNEGIE, Andrew. "Americanism versus Imperialism." *N Am Rev*, CLXVIII (1899), 1–13.

2007 CARNEGIE, Andrew. "Distant Possessions—The Parting of the Ways." *N Am Rev*, CLXVIII (1898), 239–248.

2008 CURTI, Merle E. "Bryan and World Peace." *Smith College Studies in History*, XVI, Nos. 3–4 (1931), 113–262.

2009 FREIDEL, Frank "Dissent in the Spanish-American War and the Philippine Insurrection." *Proc Mass Hist Soc*, LXXXI (1969), 167–184.

2010 HARRINGTON, Fred H. "The Anti-Imperialist Movement in the United States, 1898–1900." *Miss Val Hist Rev*, XXII (1935), 211-230.

2011 HARRINGTON, Fred H. "Literary Aspects of American Anti-Imperialism, 1898–1902." *N Eng Q*, X (1937), 650–667.

2012 HOAR, George F. *No Constitutional Power to Conquer Foreign Nations and Hold Their People in Subjection Against Their Will.* Washington, 1899.

2013 LASCH, Christopher. "The Anti-Imperialists, the Philippines, and the Inequality of Man." *J S Hist*, XXIV (1958), 319–331.

2014 MARKOWITZ, Gerald. "A Note on the Anti-Imperialist Movement of the 1890s." *Sci Soc*, XXXVII (1973), 342–345.

2015 PATERSON, Thomas G., ed. *American Imperialism and Anti-Imperialism.* New York, 1973.

2016 ROLLINS, John W. "The Anti-Imperialists and Twentieth Century American Foreign Policy." *Stud on the Left*, III (1962), 9–24.

2017 SCHURZ, Carl. "Thoughts on American Imperialism." *Century*, LVI (1898), 781–788.

2018 SMITH, Goldwin. *Commonwealth or Empire.* New York, 1902.

2019 SMITH, Robert E. "The Anti-Imperialist Crusade of Thomas M. Patterson." *Colorado Mag*, LI (1974), 28–42.

2020 STOREY, Moorfield. *Our New Departure.* Boston, 1901.

2021 STOREY, Moorfield. *What Shall We Do with Our Dependencies?* Boston, 1903.

2022 SUMNER, William G. *The Predominant Issue.* Burlington, Vt., 1901.

2023 TOMPKINS, E. Berkeley. "The Old Guard: A Study of the Anti-Imperialist Leadership." *The Historian*, XXX (1968), 366–388.

2024 TOMPKINS, E. Berkeley. "Scylla and Charybdis: The Anti-Imperialist Dilemma in the Election of 1900." *Pac Hist Rev*, XXXVI (1967), 143–161.

2025 TULCHIN, Joseph S. "The Reformer Who Would Not Succeed: The Aberrant Behavior of Edward Atkinson (1827–1905) and the Anti-Imperialist League." *Essex Inst Hist Coll*, CV (1969), 75–95.

2026 VEST, G. G. "Objections to Annexing the Philippines." *N Am Rev*, CLXVIII (1899), 112–120.

2027 WELCH, Richard E., Jr. *Imperialists vs. Anti-Imperialists: The Debate over Expansion in the 1890s.* Itasca, Ill., 1972.

2028 WELCH, Richard E., Jr. "Motives and Policy Objectives of Anti-Imperialists, 1898." *Mid-Am*, LI (1969), 119–129.

2029 WELCH, Richard E., Jr. "Opponents and Colleagues: George Frisbie Hoar and Henry Cabot Lodge, 1898–1904." *N Eng Q*, XXXIX (1966), 182–209.

2030 WELCH, Richard E., Jr. "Senator George Frisbie Hoar and the Defeat of Anti-Imperialism, 1898–1900." *The Historian*, XXVI (1964), 362–380.

2031 WILLIAMSON, Harold F. *Edward Atkinson: The Biography of an American Liberal.* Boston, 1934.

2032 WINSLOW, Erving. "The Anti-Imperialist League." *Independent*, LI (1899), 1347–1350.

2033 WINSLOW, Erving. "The Anti-Imperialist Position." *N Am Rev*, CLXXI (1900), 460–469.

5. China and the Open Door

2034 BAU, Mingchien Joshua. *The Open Door Doctrine in Relation to China.* New York, 1923.

2035 BERESFORD, Lord Charles. e Break-up of China. London, 1899.

2036 BERESFORD, Lord Charles. *The Memoirs of Admiral Lord Charles Beresford.* 2 vols. London, 1914.

2037 CAMPBELL, Charles S., Jr. "American Business Interests and the Open Door." *Far Eastern Q*, I (1949), 43–58.

2038 CAMPBELL, Charles S., Jr. *Special Business Interests and the Open Door Policy.* New Haven, Conn., 1951.

2039 DENNETT, Tyler. "The Open Door." *Empire in the East.* Ed. Joseph Barnes. New York, 1934.

2040 ESTHUS, Raymond A. "The Changing Concept of the Open Door, 1899–1910." *Miss Val Hist Rev*, XLVI (1959), 435–454.

2041 HUNT, Michael H. *Frontier Defense and the Open Door: Manchuria in Chinese-American Relations, 1895–1911.* New Haven, Conn., 1973.

2042 ISRAEL, Jerry. "For God, For China and For Yale—The Open Door in Action." *Am Hist Rev*, LXXV (1970), 796–807.

2043 McCORMICK, Thomas J. " 'A Fair Field and No Favor,' American China Policy During the McKinley Administration, 1897–1901." Doctoral dissertation, University of Wisconsin, 1960.

2044 McCORMICK, Thomas J. *China Market: America's Quest for Informal Empire, 1893–1901.* Chicago, 1967*

2045 McCORMICK, Thomas J. "American Expansion in China." *Am Hist Rev,* LXXV (1970), 1393–1396.

2046 PRESSMAN, Harvey. "Hay, Rockhill, and China's Integrity: A Reappraisal." Harvard University Center for East Asian Studies, *Papers on China,* XIII (1959), 61–79.

2047 VARG, Paul A. *The Making of a Myth: The United States and China, 1897–1912.* East Lansing, Mich., 1968.

2048 VARG, Paul A. "The Myth of the China Market, 1890–1914." *Am Hist Rev,* LXXIII (1968), 742–758.

2049 VARG, Paul A. *Open Door Diplomat: The Life of W. W. Rockhill.* Urbana, Ill., 1952.

2050 VARG, Paul A. "William Woodville Rockhill and the Open Door Notes." *J Mod Hist,* XXIV (1952), 375–380.

2051 WILLIAMS, William A. *The Tragedy of American Diplomacy.* See **110**.

2052 WILSON, James H. "America's Interests in China." *N Am Rev,* CLXVI (1898), 129–141.

2053 WRIGHT, S. F. *Hart and the Chinese Customs.* Belfast, 1950.

2054 YOUNG, Marilyn Blatt. *The Rhetoric of Empire: American China Policy, 1895–1901.* Cambridge, Mass., 1968.

Index

INDEX

INDEX

INDEX

INDEX

INDEX

INDEX

INDEX

110

INDEX

111

INDEX

INDEX

INDEX

114

INDEX

INDEX